WORLD
HISTORY SERIES ▪ ▪ ▪

The Civil Rights Movement

Titles in the World History Series

The Age of Augustus
The Age of Feudalism
The Age of Pericles
The Alamo
America in the 1960s
The American Frontier
The American Revolution
Ancient Greece
The Ancient Near East
Architecture
Aztec Civilization
The Battle of the
    Little Bighorn
The Black Death
The Byzantine Empire
Caesar's Conquest of Gaul
The California Gold Rush
The Chinese Cultural
    Revolution
The Civil Rights Movement
The Collapse of the
    Roman Republic
The Conquest of Mexico
The Crimean War
The Crusades
The Cuban Missile Crisis
The Cuban Revolution
The Early Middle Ages
Egypt of the Pharaohs
Elizabethan England
The End of the Cold War
The French and Indian War
The French Revolution
The Glorious Revolution
The Great Depression
Greek and Roman
    Mythology
Greek and Roman Science

Greek and Roman Theater
The History of Slavery
Hitler's Reich
The Hundred Years' War
The Industrial Revolution
The Inquisition
The Italian Renaissance
The Late Middle Ages
The Lewis and Clark
    Expedition
The Mexican Revolution
The Mexican War of
    Independence
Modern Japan
The Mongol Empire
The Persian Empire
The Punic Wars
The Reformation
The Relocation of the
    North American Indian
The Renaissance
The Roaring Twenties
The Roman Empire
The Roman Republic
Roosevelt and the New Deal
The Russian Revolution
Russia of the Tsars
The Scientific Revolution
The Spread of Islam
The Stone Age
Traditional Africa
Traditional Japan
The Travels of Marco Polo
Twentieth Century Science
The Wars of the Roses
The Watts Riot
Women's Suffrage

WORLD HISTORY SERIES ■■■

The Civil Rights Movement

by
John M. Dunn

Lucent Books, P.O. Box 289011, San Diego, CA 92198-9011

Library of Congress Cataloging-in-Publication Data

Dunn, John M., 1949–
    The civil rights movement / by John M. Dunn.
        p. cm. — (World history series)
    Includes bibliographical references (p.   ) and index.
    Summary: A historical overview of the movement for free-
dom and equality for blacks in the United States.
    ISBN 1-56006-310-6 (alk. paper)
    1. Afro-Americans—Civil rights—History—20th century—
Juvenile literature. 2. Civil rights movements—United States—
History—20th century—Juvenile literature. 3. United States—
Race relations—Juvenile literature. [1. Afro-Americans—Civil
rights. 2. Civil rights movements. 3. Race relations.] I. Title.
II. Series.
E185.61.D89   1998
323.1'96073—dc21   97-27443
                                                                  CIP
                                                                  AC

Copyright 1998 by Lucent Books, Inc., P.O. Box 289011,
San Diego, California 92198-9011

Printed in the U.S.A.

Contents

Foreword   6
Important Dates in the History of the
  Civil Rights Movement   8

INTRODUCTION
A Struggle to Change Hearts and Minds   10

CHAPTER 1
The Roots of the Civil Rights Movement   13

CHAPTER 2
The Long Night   29

CHAPTER 3
Black Attitudes Change   39

CHAPTER 4
The Walls of Segregation Begin to Crack   46

CHAPTER 5
The Rise of White Militant Resistance   59

CHAPTER 6
Confrontations   73

CHAPTER 7
Battle for the Ballot   89

CHAPTER 8
The Movement Splinters   100

CHAPTER 9
The Legacy of the Civil Rights Movement   112

Notes   117
For Further Reading   120
Works Consulted   121
Index   124
Picture Credits   128
About the Author   128

Foreword

Each year on the first day of school, nearly every history teacher faces the task of explaining why his or her students should study history. One logical answer to this question is that exploring what happened in our past explains how the things we often take for granted—our customs, ideas, and institutions—came to be. As statesman and historian Winston Churchill put it, "Every nation or group of nations has its own tale to tell. Knowledge of the trials and struggles is necessary to all who would comprehend the problems, perils, challenges, and opportunities which confront us today." Thus, a study of history puts modern ideas and institutions in perspective. For example, though the founders of the United States were talented and creative thinkers, they clearly did not invent the concept of democracy. Instead, they adapted some democratic ideas that had originated in ancient Greece and with which the Romans, the British, and others had experimented. An exploration of these cultures, then, reveals their very real connection to us through institutions that continue to shape our daily lives.

Another reason often given for studying history is the idea that lessons exist in the past from which contemporary societies can benefit and learn. This idea, although controversial, has always been an intriguing one for historians. Those who agree that society can benefit from the past often quote philosopher George Santayana's famous statement, "Those who cannot remember the past are condemned to repeat it." Historians who ascribe to Santayana's philosophy believe that, for example, studying the events that led up to the major world wars or other significant historical events would allow society to chart a different and more favorable course in the future.

Just as difficult as convincing students to realize the importance of studying history is the search for useful and interesting supplementary materials that present historical events in a context that can be easily understood. The volumes in Lucent Books' World History Series attempt to present a broad, balanced, and penetrating view of the march of history. Ancient Egypt's important wars and rulers, for example, are presented against the rich and colorful backdrop of Egyptian religious, social, and cultural developments. The series engages the reader by enhancing historical events with these cultural contexts. For example, in *Ancient Greece*, the text covers the role of women in that society. Slavery is discussed in *The Roman Empire*, as well as how slaves earned their freedom. The numerous and varied aspects of everyday life in these and other societies are explored in each volume of the series. Additionally, the series covers the major political, cultural, and philosophical ideas as the torch of civilization is passed from ancient Mesopotamia and Egypt, through Greece, Rome, Medieval Europe, and other world cultures, to the modern day.

The material in the series is formatted in a thorough, precise, and organized manner. Each volume offers the reader a comprehensive and clearly written overview of an important historical event or period. The topic under discussion is placed in a broad historical context. For example, *The Italian Renaissance* begins with a discussion of the High Middle Ages and the loss of central control that allowed certain Italian cities to develop artistically. The book ends by looking forward to the Reformation and interpreting the societal changes that grew out of the Renaissance. Thus, students are not only involved in an historical era, but also enveloped by the events leading up to that era and the events following it.

One important and unique feature in the World History Series is the primary and secondary source quotations that richly supplement each volume. These quotes are useful in a number of ways. First, they allow students access to sources they would not normally be exposed to because of the difficulty and obscurity of the original source. The quotations range from interesting anecdotes to farsighted cultural perspectives and are drawn from historical witnesses both past and present. Second, the quotes demonstrate how and where historians themselves derive their information on the past as they strive to reach a consensus on historical events. Lastly, all of the quotes are footnoted, familiarizing students with the citation process and allowing them to verify quotes and/or look up the original source if the quote piques their interest.

Finally, the books in the World History Series provide a detailed launching point for further research. Each book contains a bibliography specifically geared toward student research. A second, annotated bibliography introduces students to all the sources the author consulted when compiling the book. A chronology of important dates gives students an overview, at a glance, of the topic covered. Where applicable, a glossary of terms is included.

In short, the series is designed not only to acquaint readers with the basics of history, but also to make them aware that their lives are a part of an ongoing human saga. Perhaps they will then come to the same realization as famed historian Arnold Toynbee. In his monumental work, *A Study of History,* he wrote about becoming aware of history flowing through him in a mighty current, and of his own life "welling like a wave in the flow of this vast tide."

Important Dates in the History of the Civil Rights Movement

1619	1700	1725	1750	1775	1800	1825

1619
African slaves arrive in North America.

1863
Emancipation Proclamation frees Southern slaves.

1865
Thirteenth Amendment abolishing slavery ratified.

1866
Congress passes nation's first Civil Rights Act, making former slaves citizens of the United States; Fourteenth Amendment ratified, affirming U.S. citizenship for blacks; also gives blacks equal protection of the law.

1870
Fifteenth Amendment banning race discrimination in voting ratified.

1875
Congress passes Civil Rights Act banning discrimination in public places and on juries; first Jim Crow law enacted in Tennessee.

1877
Reconstruction ends.

1883
U.S. Supreme Court rules part of the 1875 Civil Rights Act unconstitutional.

1896
Plessy v. Ferguson's "separate but equal" doctrine defines race relations in America.

1882–1901
Lynchings become epidemic in the South.

1906
W. E. B. Du Bois launches the Niagara Movement.

1910
National Association for the Advancement of Colored People founded.

1912
Woodrow Wilson segregates federal workforce.

1917–1919
Blacks subject to racist policies in the U.S. armed forces during WWI; outbreak of postwar race riots.

1933
Margold Report outlines legal attack on "separate but equal."

1935
Baltimore court rules Donald Murray must be admitted to white law school.

1938
Supreme Court rules that Lloyd Lionel Gaines must be admitted to the University of Missouri Law School.

1941
Franklin Roosevelt issues order to ban discrimination in defense plants; United States enters WWII.

1946
Harry Truman's Committee on Civil Rights recommends new emphasis on civil rights for blacks.

1948
Truman issues order to desegregate U.S. armed forces.

1950
Supreme Court rules in *Sweatt v. Painter* and *McLaurin v. Oklahoma* that segregation of law school program is unconstitutional.

1954
Plessy v. Ferguson is overturned by *Brown v. Board of Education*.

1955
Second *Brown* decision calls for school desegregation; Emmett Till and other NAACP organizers murdered in Mississippi; Rosa Parks arrested in Montgomery, sparking bus boycott; Martin Luther King emerges as spokesperson for the civil rights movement.

1956
Southern Manifesto protesting desegregation made public; Supreme Court outlaws segregated seating on Montgomery buses.

1957
Arkansas governor Faubus calls out National Guard to prevent nine black students from entering Little Rock High School; Dwight Eisenhower sends one thousand army paratroopers to restore order and escort black students to class.

1960
Four students stage sit-in at Woolworth department store in Greensboro, North Carolina; Student Non-violent Coordinating Committee founded; massive sit-ins take place across the South.

1961
Freedom Rides provoke violence in Montgomery; Interstate Commerce Commission bans segregated facilities at bus terminals and rail stations.

1962
James Meredith's enrollment at the University of Mississippi ignites biggest conflict between the federal government and southerners since the Civil War.

1963
Civil rights groups commence major desegregation campaign in Birmingham; NAACP field secretary Medgar Evers is assassinated; 250,000 demonstrators march on Washington; Alabama governor George Wallace attempts to prevent desegregation of public schools; bomb kills four black children in a Birmingham church; John F. Kennedy is assassinated.

1964–1968
Summers of black rioting in major U.S. cities.

1964
Twenty-fourth Amendment banning poll taxes ratified; Lyndon Johnson signs into law a sweeping civil rights law; SCLC and SNCC launch Mississippi Freedom Project; death of three civil rights workers alarms the nation.

1965
King and others lead voter registration demonstration in Selma; violent response to King's Selma-to-Montgomery march commands national sympathy and massive federal support from Johnson; in
July, Johnson signs Voting Rights Act; Malcolm X is assassinated; Johnson initiates federal "affirmative action" policy.

1966
James Meredith is shot during his Walk Against Fear; King leads march through Chicago; SNCC and CORE adopt Black Power philosophies.

1968
Martin Luther King is assassinated; Johnson signs 1968 Civil Rights Act; Ralph Abernathy leads Poor People's March on Washington.

1971
In *Swann v. Charlotte-Mecklenburg Board of Education*, Supreme Court holds that federal courts can order busing to desegregate schools.

1995
Supreme Court holds in *Missouri v. Jenkins* that a district federal judge may not order a magnet school plan to be imposed on the Kansas City school system; the Million Man March takes place in Washington, D.C.

A Struggle to Change Hearts and Minds

"One day historians will record this movement as one of the most significant epics of our heritage."[1] Martin Luther King Jr. spoke these words in 1962 about the modern civil rights movement that began in 1954 and lasted more than two decades. This drive was a particularly noteworthy phase of a much older, ongoing struggle in which hundreds of thousands of Americans participated to persuade the nation and its institutions to officially recognize and protect civil rights long denied black Americans.

Civil rights are entitlements guaranteed by the U.S. government that include the right to vote, own property, receive equal protection of the law, and enjoy freedom from involuntary servitude. But for more than a century, these rights generally applied to white Americans only: Many of the nation's blacks, particularly those in the American South, were routinely denied them. Instead, racism, hatred, ignorance, injustice—the bitter legacies of slavery and civil war—imposed upon African Americans a second-class status.

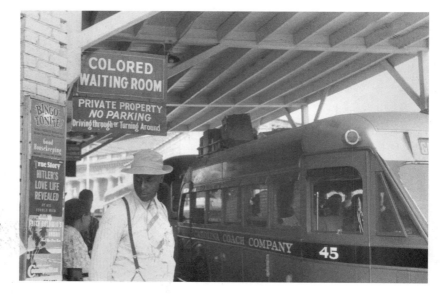

Blacks wait for their bus in an area designated as "colored." Even though blacks had ostensibly won their freedom after the Civil War, they continued to experience segregation and discrimination.

Members of the Congress of Racial Equality march in memory of four black girls who were killed in a Birmingham, Alabama, church bombing in 1965. Such violence against blacks was rampant throughout the South.

But change did come. Landmark legal decisions by the U.S. Supreme Court beginning in the 1930s legitimized the movement. Historian C. Vann Woodward notes that other forces aided the crusade,

> including the pressure and propaganda organizations for civil rights—both Negro and white, Northern and Southern. There were also executive orders of Presidents, acts of Congress, policy decisions of federal agencies, actions by labor unions, professional organizations, churches, corporation executives, and educational leaders.[2]

In addition, two world wars helped pave a way for American blacks by altering the social, economic, and political conditions in the United States in ways that catalyzed the modern movement. Many African Americans who participated in these global military conflicts felt a special urgency to fight for their own freedom once they returned to the United States.

Television—a new technology in the 1950s—played a major role, too. Images of whites brutally beating and teargassing nonviolent civil rights marchers revealed to the world that America had not yet lived up to its professed democratic ideals. Such news reports embarrassed the federal government and spurred it to take action on behalf of blacks and other minorities.

Television also gave people around the world a chance to see and hear spellbinding orators such as King enunciate the noble and universal aspirations of the movement. Such exposure helped generate worldwide support for the efforts of civil rights workers.

Though much of the civil rights movement was carried out peaceably, violent confrontations, beatings, firebombings, and killings also occurred. White mobs, terrorists, and even law enforcement officers frequently resorted to violence to thwart the progress of the movement and to keep blacks "in their place." And angry and frustrated blacks bent on revenge and retaliation sometimes initiated violence against whites.

Though racial tensions still exist in America, the civil rights movement largely accomplished what it set out to do. African Americans and other minorities can now legally exercise the civil rights promised them at the end of the Civil War. Ironically, the very same governments and institutions that once denied these rights to black Americans are now their chief enforcers.

Changed too are the hearts and minds of millions of ordinary Americans who have quietly accepted the inevitability of having fellow citizens with different racial and ethnic backgrounds. Most are repelled by the racism of the past—a racism whose roots are deeply entangled in the history of the nation.

1 The Roots of the Civil Rights Movement

When the first black slaves arrived in Virginia in 1619 civil rights were not an issue. Seized by force and torn from their loved ones, millions of Africans were shipped in filthy, disease-ridden ships across the Atlantic Ocean to labor in the New World, and slavery was an established institution for the next 250 years.

In 1857, the U.S. Supreme Court ruled that slaves had no rights "which any white man was bound to respect."[3] Families were often separated and sold. American slaves

This illustration shows the conditions aboard a slave ship in 1860. The inhumane treatment aboard these ships resulted in the deaths of many blacks.

Lincoln signs the Emancipation Proclamation in 1863. Although the proclamation freed slaves in the southern states, it did not eliminate slavery in the states that had remained loyal to the Union.

could not testify in court against those who treated them cruelly. In addition, they were generally not permitted to buy their freedom as were slaves elsewhere in the New World.

Obliteration of Slavery

Though slavery of African Americans was legal, many whites across the nation—including the South—were appalled by the practice and took part in a major antislavery campaign that helped start the American Civil War in 1861.

Though ending slavery was not a goal for the North at the beginning of the war, it became one in 1863 with Abraham Lincoln's Emancipation Proclamation—a presidential order that freed all slaves in the rebelling states. But the decree did nothing to stop slavery in the slave states that remained loyal to the Union.

Slavery's final end came in 1865, when Americans ratified the Thirteenth Amendment to the Constitution shortly after the

end of the Civil War. Suddenly 4 million former slaves were free. But free to do what? Most black people were penniless and illiterate. They owned no property and had few marketable skills. As Benjamin G. Humphreys, Mississippi's new governor, told the Mississippi legislature in 1865, "The Negro is free, whether we like it or not. . . . To be free, however, does not make a citizen or entitle him to social or political equality with the white man."[4]

Humphrey's assessment mirrored an attitude rampant throughout the South. "Wherever I go—the street, the shop, the house, the hotel, or the steamboat—I hear people talk in such a way as to indicate that they are yet unable to conceive of the Negro as possessing any rights at all,"[5] wrote Carl Schurz, a Lincoln aide sent to study the condition of the South after the war.

But many northerners also had doubts about granting equality to blacks. Some, like Abraham Lincoln, believed the white race would never accept them as equals. During the Civil War, Lincoln often discussed with advisers the possibility of sending freed blacks to Africa or another country such as Panama or the West Indies, rather than trying to integrate them into American society.

Thus, the entire nation now had a new question to resolve: Did freedom entitle blacks to equal treatment under the law?

A Bitter Legacy

The Civil War devastated the South. Everywhere, homes, farms, and cities were in ruins. Crops and livestock were destroyed. The South's economic, political, military, and social systems were demolished. Hunger, disease, and despair haunted whites and blacks alike.

Most white southerners hated the North with a single-minded passion. Their bitterness stemmed not only from the sting and disgrace of military defeat: They also feared that blacks, now free, would take revenge in a massive uprising.

Lincoln wanted to lessen this resentment and anxiety by taking a lenient approach to southern reconstruction and reestablished reunification. His successor, Andrew Johnson, agreed. But this policy was a flawed one for southern blacks. In 1866 and 1867, provisional southern

Freed slaves in Charleston, South Carolina, take a meal from a makeshift soup kitchen. Many blacks were left homeless and unemployed after the Civil War.

governments, set up by Johnson, took advantage of federal leniency to reimpose conditions of near slavery on the freed slaves with special state laws called Black Codes.

The Black Codes

Though they varied from state to state, all Black Codes had a common purpose: to control southern blacks and prevent them from full participation in the legal, social, and political aspects of southern life.

In some states, the codes gave freed blacks the right to give evidence in court, own land, attend school, and marry. But they also limited how much land African Americans could own and often forbade them to work as mechanics or artisans. The codes also gave law enforcement officials the right to arrest unemployed blacks as vagrants and turn them over to white planters—often their former

A Sense of a Divided Self

In his book The Souls of Black Folk, *W. E. B. Du Bois argues that black Americans possessed a unique sense of personal identity forged in slavery that set them apart from the mainstream of white American society.*

"The Negro is . . . born with a veil, and gifted with second-sight in the American world,—a world which yields him no true self-consciousness, but only lets him see himself through the revelation of the other world. It is a peculiar sensation, this double-consciousness, the sense of always looking at one's self through the eyes of others, of measuring one's soul by the tape of a world that looks on in amused contempt and pity. One ever feels his twoness,—an American, a Negro; two souls, two thoughts, two unreconciled strivings; two warring ideals in one dark body, whose dogged strength alone keeps it from being torn asunder.

The history of the American Negro is the history of this . . . longing to . . . merge his double self into a better and truer self. In this merging he wishes neither of the older selves to be lost. He would not Africanize America, for America has too much to teach the world and Africa. He would not bleach his Negro soul in a flood of white Americanism, for he knows that Negro blood has a message for the world. He simply wishes to make it possible for a man to be both a Negro and an American, without being cursed and spit upon by his fellows, without having the doors of Opportunity closed roughly in his face."

Like many other southern cities, Charleston, South Carolina, was devastated by the Civil War.

masters—to work off their sentences. Curfews were set for blacks. They could not own guns or buy alcoholic drinks. Almost everywhere in the South, African Americans were forbidden to sit on juries, vote, or run for office.

Congress Takes Control

Infuriated by the codes and Johnson's permissive stance, Congress wrested control of the South from the executive branch and imposed its own harsher form of reconstruction. One of its first acts was to nullify the Black Codes with the passage of the Civil Rights Act of April 9, 1866. This act, the first of its kind, officially granted African Americans U.S. citizenship. As citizens, they were now enti-

tled, on paper, to the same rights and federal protection as whites.

In the event that future lawmakers repealed the Civil Rights Act, Congress also passed the Fourteenth Amendment to the Constitution, underscoring the Civil Rights Act by making black Americans citizens of the nation and of the state in which they lived. It also granted all citizens full and equal protection under the law.

Next, Congress required that southern states ratify the Fourteenth Amendment as a condition for readmittance to the Union. When all except Tennessee refused to do so, Congress reacted angrily. In 1867 it divided the South into five military districts and imposed martial law. Once again, it demanded that southerners ratify the amendment. By 1870, most southern states had complied and been readmitted.

Northern Jim Crow

"[T]he Northern Negro was made painfully and constantly aware that he lived in a society dedicated to the doctrine of white supremacy and Negro inferiority. [Whites] firmly believed that the Negroes were incapable of being assimilated politically, socially, or physically into white society. They made sure in numerous ways that the Negro understood his 'place' and that he was severely confined to it. One of these ways was segregation, and with the backing of legal and extra-legal codes, the system permeated all aspects of Negro life in the free states by 1860.

Negroes were often segregated in housing. Whites of South Boston boasted in 1847 that 'not a single colored family' lived among them. Boston had her 'Nigger Hill' and her 'New Guinea,' Cincinnati her 'Little Africa,' and New York and Philadelphia their comparable ghettoes—for which Richmond, Charleston, New Orleans, and St. Louis had no counterparts."

During the period of military occupation, federal officials encouraged southerners of both races to register to vote for new state governments and federal office-holders. Under the protection of Union troops, southern blacks were quick to take advantage of this new opportunity. By September 1867, 703,000 blacks had registered, compared with 627,000 whites.

Southern Anger and Fear Intensifies

The congressional campaign to register blacks infuriated southern whites. For one thing, they resented ceding political power to a race they considered inferior. They also feared that blacks would use their newfound political strength to retaliate against whites. And southern whites were especially resentful that as black voting strength grew, Congress deprived 150,000 southerners of the right to vote as punishment for their participation in the Confederacy.

Southern blacks invariably voted for the Republican Party—the party of Lincoln—which was universally hated by white southerners. Despite efforts by whites to keep them from the polls, blacks helped elect Republican state governments throughout the South. They also contributed to making a Republican, Ulysses S. Grant, the next president.

Southern blacks also set another precedent. Hundreds of African Americans—along with sympathetic white Republicans who had moved to the South—were elected to political office. For the first time, southern blacks held positions of power in county and state governments. Twenty-two won congressional seats in Washington.

In 1868, a Republican-dominated Congress—realizing the value of black voters in the South—passed the Fifteenth Amendment to the Constitution, upholding a black man's right to vote. In 1870 the amendment was ratified.

This rise in black and Republican power alarmed and frightened white southerners. They were also dismayed by the appearance of Loyal Leagues, political groups organized by northerners to recruit blacks for the Republican Party and urge them to denounce white southerners and the Democratic Party. Southern hatred intensified when Republican-controlled state governments created organized patrols made up of armed black men to serve as keepers of the peace in the war-torn South. Whites were now convinced that the long-feared black uprising was about to erupt.

Finally, many southern whites were also convinced that northerners were hypocritical in their handling of racial matters. Historian Tim Jacobson writes that white resistance escalated as a result of "radical Northern attempts to elevate black Southerners to social and political equality with white men in the South—but not in the North."[6]

The Rise of White Vigilantism

White southerners lashed out. As early as 1866, numerous white militias were formed bearing names such as the Ku Klux Klan, the Red Shirts, and the Pale Faces. Cultivating an image of mystery, disguised in hideous costumes, and based on a mixture of secret initiation, ritual, and violence, the vigilante groups terrorized, beat, and murdered blacks and also whites suspected of cooperating with Republicans and "leaguers."

The most fearsome vigilante group was the Ku Klux Klan. Observes Tim Jacobson:

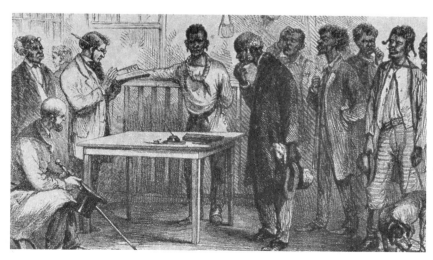

Blacks exercise their right to vote in Richmond, Virginia, in 1871. The Fifteenth Amendment secured this right for black men.

Terror was the tool used by Klansmen. Riding on horseback to the homes of blacks and claiming to be the ghosts of Confederate soldiers, Klansmen soon resorted to deadly tools. Hangings, shootings, arson, drowning—all were inflicted by Klan members on blacks [and whites sympathetic to blacks or the Republican cause].[7]

During one of the Klan's rampages, a U.S. Army officer in Texas observed, "The murder of Negroes is so common as to render it impossible to keep accurate accounts of them."[8] In South Carolina, fear of Klan reprisals guaranteed that no jury would convict an accused Klansman. Those who testified against a Klansman faced the likelihood of being murdered. By 1871 the Klan's reign of fear was so widespread that President Grant had to order federal troops into nine South Carolina counties to protect federal judges and jurors from harassment and intimidation.

Grant had taken this step under the recently enacted Ku Klux Klan laws, which penalized states where vigilante groups violated the Fourteenth and Fifteenth Amendments. For instance, a county could be fined five thousand dollars if a resident was killed by a mob. Punishment was also meted out to anyone wearing the

An illustration depicts two Ku Klux Klan members in their characteristic white hoods. Upset with blacks' new-found freedoms, many white southerners joined antiblack organizations such as the Klan.

In an illustration entitled "Of Course He Wants to Vote the Democratic Ticket," white southerners defy laws guaranteeing blacks the vote by threatening a man with death if he votes Republican.

Klan costume or other disguise. Many Klansmen were prosecuted, convicted, and jailed for committing violent crimes. These punitive measures, along with a growing public disapproval of terror, helped bring on the official disbanding of the Klan in 1873.

More Civil Rights Laws

Congress did more for African Americans than rein in white terrorist groups. It also passed the Civil Rights Act of 1875. This measure gave "citizens of every race and color" the right to "equal enjoyment of the accommodations of inns, public conveyances on land and water, theaters and other places of public amusement."[9]

Meanwhile, African Americans were also taking cautious steps on their own.

Many joined a new group called the National Equal Rights League, whose goal was "to destroy restrictions which prevent colored people from entering libraries, colleges, lecture rooms, military academies, jury boxes, churches, theaters, street cars and from voting."[10]

Most newly freed blacks, however, were too timid or intimidated to assert their rights. In fact, to allay white hostility and fears, some black leaders openly professed they were interested only in obtaining civil rights and not interacting with whites socially.

All too soon they would have neither.

The End of Reconstruction

Despite the federal crackdown on the Klan and similar groups, white terror

Klan Power in North Carolina

Eyewitness: A Living Documentary of the African American Contribution to American History contains an excerpt of a statement from Colonel George W. Kirk of the North Carolina state troops about the Ku Klux Klan's brazen display of power in North Carolina in 1871.

"I have spoken of their having the law and the courts all on their side. The juries were made up of Ku-Klux, and it was impossible for any of the loyal people [to the Union] to get justice before the courts. Not less than fifty or sixty persons have been killed by the Ku-Klux in the State, besides some three or four hundred whippings, and there has never been a man convicted that I have heard of. Out of all those that I arrested, against whom there was good proof as could possibly be given, enough to convict anybody before twelve honest men, I do not think one has ever been tried. They know very well when they commit these depredations that they will be cleared, and it just makes it that much worse for the loyal people. If they prosecute them for debt or for anything else they fail. Colored men cannot get justice, cannot get their hard earned money. They agree to give them part of the crop, and about the time of the harvest they charge them with something and run them off. They dare not say a word."

effectively weakened Republican strength in the South and enabled Democrats to regain political power. In 1870 Democrats had recaptured control of state governments in Tennessee, Virginia, North Carolina, and Georgia. The final blow to Republican power came as the result of the disputed presidential election of 1876, which found Democrats and Republicans accusing each other of election fraud and refusing to concede defeat. Finally, a majority Republican commission awarded the election to Republican Rutherford B. Hayes and Democrats won a concession to end military occupation in the South.

In 1877 federal troops left the South: Reconstruction was now over. Many blacks feared that in the troops' absence southern whites would immediately reverse the gains they had made.

But this did not happen right away. Many southern whites had grown accustomed to blacks' having greater equality. They were also mindful of federal laws that protected African Americans. Even though segregation and racism persisted, southern blacks held on to their modest gains for almost two decades. During these years, many visitors to the South were astonished to see blacks and whites attending lectures and public performances together. The two races rode the same trains in Florida, Georgia, and the Carolinas. And in areas of Mississippi, blacks and whites dined in the same restaurants and bars, though at separate tables.

Southern whites' reactions to this limited level of integration, however, were increasingly polarized.

Southern Racial Views

Southern liberals, for example, championed civil rights for blacks. A small group of writers, journalists, professors, and even many former Confederate officers openly favored broad constitutional rights for African Americans. Their position was considered extreme by most other whites.

For the most part, the South's conservatives—mainly its upper-class, wealthy plantation owners—believed that as community leaders they had a responsibility to help educate African Americans. Though many planters were racists, they saw no reason to publicly humiliate and suppress blacks. As one South Carolina writer put it, "The old slave owner . . . feels no desire to maltreat and brow-beat and spit upon the colored man. He feels no opposition to the education and elevation of the black man in the scale of civilized life."[11]

But this did not mean that planters advocated equality for blacks. Often their

A Reconstruction-era illustration depicts blacks serving alongside whites on a jury. Many blacks feared that such rights would be revoked with the end of Reconstruction.

desire to assist blacks was motivated at least as much by self-interest as altruism. For one thing, industrialization had begun in the postwar South. This meant that all workers—black and white—needed better education and training. Plantation owners also tried to win favor with blacks in order to pull them away from the Republican Party. When persuasion failed to sway votes, economic reprisals often succeeded. Writes Tim Jacobson, "It was the white man who still owned the land, and the black man who was the tenant. The threat of eviction forced many blacks into voting Democratic or not voting at all."[12]

A third group of whites had no misgivings about humiliating and suppressing blacks. They were hate-mongering, mostly poor, uneducated white farmers. Resentful of their own poverty and lowly status, these whites tried to elevate themselves at the expense of African Americans. C. Vann Woodward describes these haters of blacks as "fanatics of the South, who . . . would wage aggressive war on the Negro, strip him of basic rights guaranteed him by the Constitution, ostracize him, humiliate him, and rob him of elemental human dignity."[13]

For several years following the departure of troops from the South, the planters dominated race relations in the South. But as the nineteenth century drew to a close, a new twist in national politics changed the status of blacks for the worse.

The Populists

During the 1890s, a new national political party, the Populist Party, challenged both the Republican and Democratic Parties with appeals to farmers and working-class Americans everywhere.

In particular, Populists revolted against the economic and political power of wealthy insurance and railroad companies, business monopolies, and corrupt city governments. They also demanded radical changes in how the national economy operated to make it easier for farmers to pay off debts.

For the good of the nation, Populists urged whites and blacks to forget their racial differences, band together, and oppose the big money interests of America. In 1892 Populist leader Tom Watson told a gathering of black and white farmers at Raleigh, North Carolina, why he believed the rich and powerful favored keeping the races segregated: "You [black and white farmers] are kept apart that you may be separately fleeced of your earnings. You are made to hate each other because in that hatred is rested the keystone of the financial despotism which enslaves you both."[14]

Efforts to Unite Races

Populists also tried to entice blacks to their ranks with special promises. For instance, they supported African American candidacy for political office. In addition, Populists pledged to end the practice in some southern states of using black convicts as free labor for businesses.

Though persuading the races to unite was difficult, Populists made some progress. "While the movement was at the peak of zeal the two races had surprised each other and astonished their opponents by the harmony they achieved and the good will with which they co-operated,"[15] writes C. Vann Woodward.

In fact, the degree of racial unity achieved by the Populists startled conservative, wealthy southern whites, who dominated the Democratic Party and feared the Populist agenda. "The Populist crusade swept through the Southern countryside in the early 1890s, striking fear in the ranks of the Democrats and causing them to employ desperate counter measures,"[16] observes historian Dewey W. Grantham.

The Democrats now resolved to beat back the threat of populism by any means possible. This determination included stuffing ballot boxes and either bribing or intimidating black voters to vote against Populist candidates. Though the planters had earlier shunned overt racism, their rhetoric became blatantly racist in an effort to divide their opponents. "White Democrats charged that the unholy alliance of blacks and whites would corrupt Southern morality and return the hated Republican party to power,"[17] notes historian Robert A. Calvert.

Terror from the Loyal League

In this passage from his book The Angry Scar, *Pulitzer Prize–winning editor Hodding Carter describes the role the Loyal Leagues played in fostering terror and violence during Reconstruction in the South.*

"The Leagues were skillfully designed to remind the Negroes of their new importance and their obligations to the Republican party as the author of their freedom. They were organized in secret, mumbo-jumbo, ritualistic lodges. The password was the four L's—*Lincoln, Liberty, Loyal, League.* Elaborate prayers and incantations enlivened the meetings. The flag, the Bible, and copies of the Declaration of Independence and the Constitution were prominently displayed. . . .

The Loyal Leagues fanned the fires of racial discord. Their assemblies were characterized by denunciations of the Southern whites. Negroes who through loyalty to their former masters were reluctant to turn against them or become Republicans were threatened with death; many were badly beaten and some were murdered. The Loyal Leagues in places organized military units and drilled along the highways; inevitably clashes between the armed Negroes and armed whites were frequent.

White and Negro organizers promised that the land of the white Confederates would be confiscated and divided among the Negroes."

These race-baiting tactics worked. As apathy and internal bickering weakened the Populist crusade, many poor whites turned against their black allies and blamed them for the movement's failure. Soon blacks found themselves shunned by both Democrats and former Populists. Moreover, African Americans also found that the federal courts were forsaking them.

Reversals in the Courts

The first major blow came when the Supreme Court ruled that a provision of the 1875 Civil Rights Act was unconstitutional. Though this act guaranteed blacks access to public accommodations, many southern whites continued to openly discriminate against African Americans. Across the South, blacks were routinely turned away from public places such as hotels and first-class compartments of trains. Some African Americans fought back in court, demanding that their rights be upheld. Various related lawsuits were collectively known as the Civil Rights Cases of 1883, eventually reaching the Supreme Court.

The Court ruled against the plaintiffs, arguing that the Fourteenth Amendment outlawed only acts of discrimination by state governments—not those of individuals. Thus, said the Court, owners and operators of public accommodations were free to discriminate.

Outraged by the Court's decision, northern and midwestern state governments passed laws to protect their black citizens. But no southern state followed suit.

Plessy v. Ferguson

The Court's ruling in another suit in 1896 represented an even bigger setback for blacks. This dispute arose when a Louisiana man named Homer A. Plessy challenged the constitutionality of the state's separate railroad car law. One day, Plessy (who was one-eighth black) was arrested when he refused to leave a whites-only compartment on the East Louisiana Railway in New Orleans. He later sued the railway company, arguing that his right to equal protection under the Fourteenth Amendment had been violated.

But in *Plessy v. Ferguson* the nation's highest court upheld the Louisiana law. It ruled that the state law did not discriminate because it provided "separate but equal" seating for both races. The law merely offered "race distinction." And since it guaranteed all Louisiana citizens "access" to public places it did not violate the federal law.

As a new standard for race relations was being defined by the Court, white lawmakers in the South hastened to pass state laws that separated the races and stripped blacks of first-class citizenship.

Meanwhile, the racism legitimized by these federal court decisions paralleled racist trends that spread across the nation.

National Racism

By the end of the century, the United States had acquired overseas territories consisting of Hawaii, Guam, Puerto Rico, and the Philippines. Supporters of American imperialism argued that English-speaking white Americans were superior to the inhabitants

Blacks punch holes in metal bars for the battleship Illinois *during the Spanish-American War. Although blacks participated in the American economy, many whites wanted to deny them the right to participate politically.*

of these foreign lands and therefore had a right, if not a duty, to spread American culture and power abroad. Many agreed with Senator Albert J. Beveridge, who argued in 1898 that

> God has not been preparing the English-speaking and Teutonic [Germanic] peoples for a thousand years for nothing but vain and idle self-contemplation and self-admiration. No! He has made us the master organizers of the world to establish system when chaos reigns. He has made us adept in government that we may administer government among savages and servile peoples.[18]

Such rhetoric convinced many Americans to reexamine the racial situation in the South. If white American racial superiority was valid overseas, they reasoned that suppression of other minorities was justified at home. As inferiors, why should blacks be granted the rights of whites?

Economic woes were also causing many northerners to have second thoughts about their earlier criticism of how white southerners treated blacks. By now, hundreds of thousands of southern blacks had migrated to northern cities looking for work and better opportunities. As competition for jobs increased, racial tensions mounted and northern sympathy for blacks dwindled.

Losing Ground

In the late 1890s, southern blacks watched with growing apprehension as their former supporters abandoned them. No longer could they count on help from sympathetic northerners, the federal courts, the radical Populists, or even the paternalistic planters. Without these inhibiting forces, the racist element of southern society was free to exert its will unimpeded. Making matters worse, most factionalized southern whites put aside their differences stemming from the Populist period. Many turned to scapegoating blacks as responsible for the disunity in the first place.

As the nineteenth century drew to a close, whites across the South closed ranks and launched their assault. Thus began for blacks an era of lost liberties, degradation, fear, and woe known as "the Long Night."

2 The Long Night

One of the first moves against southern blacks was disenfranchisement, or removal of their right to vote. This step satisfied conservative white Democrats because it reduced the number of Republican voters. And racists were glad to see blacks deprived of a right that entailed equal power for blacks and whites.

Disenfranchisement was not a simple matter, however. The Fifteenth Amendment forbids denying anyone the vote based on race. But southern politicians used other methods to achieve the same end, including the use of the poll tax, a levy on voting. Though applied to blacks and whites alike, this measure effectively targeted African Americans, who were more often poor and thus more often unable to pay the tax, which averaged anywhere from one to several dollars.

Literacy tests were also used as discriminatory devices. These exams required an applicant to read and explain difficult passages from documents such as state laws. They were purposely hard—if not impossible—for black applicants to pass. Some registrars, for example, required blacks to recite the entire U.S. Constitution.

As a black man votes, white men look on with obvious resentment and derision.

The slightest error in pronunciation or interpretation of the text could be grounds for disqualification.

Whites, on the other hand, generally faced easy questions, or none at all. Many avoided the tests entirely thanks to a grandfather clause that excluded anyone whose grandfather had voted prior to the Civil War. Some southern states also passed property requirements and so-called good character clauses that gave election officials extra power to discriminate against African Americans.

Those few blacks who did manage to register to vote faced yet another hurdle. In many places in the South, the Democratic Party declared that its primaries—elections to determine candidates for the general election—were private affairs for "whites only"; black opinion and participation was virtually squelched.

A Wave of Violence

Away from the county courthouse, whites found other forms of intimidation. Black workers merely overheard talking about registering to vote could find themselves suddenly thrown out of work by an angry boss. Self-employed black farmers and merchants who voted soon discovered that banks cut off their credit or suppliers stopped further shipments.

Violence was also common. In many areas of the Deep South—particularly in the cotton states such as Alabama and Mississippi—white roughnecks beat African Americans who tried to register. Black homes and barns were set ablaze in the middle of the night, and local sheriffs often responded by arresting blacks for the arson of their own property.

Such harassment and brutality were part of a wave of violence taking place during the Long Night. In many rural areas of the South, African Americans were beaten and killed for committing even the slightest infractions against the southern social code. Merely failing to say "sir" to a white man sometimes invited severe violence.

Southern blacks constantly lived in fear of becoming a victim of a lynching, an execution by hanging carried out by a white mob. A longtime frontier style of justice in the South, lynchings became epidemic during the Long Night: Vigilante groups hanged more than two thousand blacks between 1882 and 1901.

The disenfranchisement campaign worked. Black voting strength, and thus black political power, dwindled significantly during the 1890s. In Louisiana, for example, the number of black voters dropped from 130,334 to 1,342 between 1896 and 1904. Fledgling African American participation in government died out. In 1901 the last black congressman from the South, North Carolina's George H. White, delivered this bitter farewell in the House of Representatives:

This, Mr. Chairman, is the Negroes' temporary farewell to the American Congress; but let me say, Phoenix-like he will rise up some day and come again. These parting words are in behalf of an outraged, heart-broken, bruised and bleeding, but God-fearing people, faithful, industrious, loyal people—rising people, full of potential force. . . .

I am pleading for the life, liberty, the future happiness, and manhood suffrage of one-eighth of the entire population of the United States.[19]

Widening the Goals of Jim Crow

Southern whites were not content with disenfranchisement. They also unleashed a barrage of restrictive laws, rules, and regulations aimed at segregating blacks from whites. These measures were called Jim Crow laws (a name derived from an old minstrel show). Similar to Black Codes during Reconstruction, Jim Crow laws were meant to keep blacks from achieving equality with whites.

Separate public schools for blacks and whites were set up across the South. Water fountains and restrooms were designated for whites and "colored." Railroad, streetcar, and steamboat companies maintained separate compartments. In some factories and businesses, the two races worked in different areas and drew wages at separate pay windows. One South Carolina mill even required blacks and whites to look out different windows during breaks. Southern hospitals maintained segregated rooms and

A sign advertises a rally against lynching. Over two thousand blacks were lynched by white mobs between 1882 and 1901.

An illustration depicting a school for black children in Charleston, South Carolina, shows the overcrowded conditions and lack of desks typical of such schools.

separate blood supplies for patients. When southerners died, their bodies were taken to segregated funeral parlors and buried in "racially pure" graveyards.

Although the South was the home of slavery, this kind of strict physical segregation was something new. Before the Civil War, the supervision of slaves required that whites live in proximity to blacks. On plantations the races lived and worked together at close quarters. Black servants cooked meals for whites and cleaned their homes. Many white children had black nannies and played with black children. The two races frequently attended the same churches.

But Jim Crow practices destroyed these old patterns and changed the South into the most racially divided region in the nation.

Separate and Unequal

Segregation did more than keep the races apart. It imposed unequal and degrading conditions on African Americans. Negro schools, for example, invariably were less well funded and supplied than white schools. As a result, they were generally crowded, poorly staffed, and underequipped. Public libraries either refused to serve blacks or provided them with separate and inferior facilities. Blacks could not eat in most white-owned restaurants; instead they were required to stand at rear entrances and place their orders. White merchants refused to allow black patrons to try on articles of clothing before they purchased them. White-owned hotels in the South were off-limits to black travelers.

The Birth of a Movement

Despite all these hardships, many African Americans held on to their dream of achieving equality. But they disagreed on how to proceed: Some favored aggressively challenging Jim Crow laws to give blacks greater opportunities; others feared that integration, and assimilation into white culture, would cause

---

Tennessee's Jim Crow Law in Education (1901)

Civil Rights and the American Negro, *edited by Albert P. Blaustein and Robert L. Zangrando, provides this portion of a Tennessee Jim Crow law.*

"An act to prohibit the co-education of the white and colored races and to prohibit the white and colored races from attending the same schools, academies, colleges or other places of learning in this state.

Section 1. *Be it enacted by the General Assembly of the State of Tennessee,* That hereafter it shall be unlawful for any school, academy, college or other place of learning to allow white and colored persons to attend the same school, academy, college or other place of learning.

Sec. 2. *Be it further enacted,* That it shall be unlawful for any teacher, professor or educator in the State, in any college, academy or school of learning, to allow the white and colored races to attend the same school or for any teacher or educator, or other person to instruct or teach both the white and colored races in the same class, school or college building, or in any other place or places of learning, or allow or permit the same to be done with their knowledge, consent or procurement.

Sec. 3. *Be it further enacted,* That any person or persons violating this Act or any of its provisions, when convicted shall be fined for each offense fifty ($50) dollars and imprisoned not less than thirty days nor more than six months, at the discretion of the Court."

African Americans to lose their own black identity and culture.

Some leaders suggested that blacks should advance carefully and cautiously in their demands for more opportunities in American society to avoid provoking a white backlash. Booker T. Washington, founder of the vocational Tuskeegee Institute in Alabama, stressed that blacks should be temporarily content to learn manual skills, and not impinge on the professional world dominated by whites. He made this point in an 1895 speech in Atlanta:

> In the great leap from slavery to freedom . . . the masses of us are to live by the production of our hands. . . . We shall prosper . . . as we learn to dignify and glorify common labor. . . . It is at the bottom of life we must begin, and not at the top.[20]

Washington went so far as to say that for the moment freed blacks should not aggressively press for desegregation and civil rights.

Why wait? responded W. E. B. Du Bois, a fiery opponent of Washington. Du Bois—the first black to receive a Ph.D. from Harvard—urged African Americans to demand their rights now. Hadn't they waited for hundreds of years already? he asked.

Booker T. Washington recommended that blacks approach racism and discrimination with patience. Washington believed that if blacks worked hard they would eventually prosper.

W. E. B. Du Bois encouraged blacks to fight to obtain the rights they deserved. Du Bois despised the advice of black leaders such as Booker T. Washington, who recommended patience and endurance.

Frustrated by the slow pace of change, Du Bois and other African American leaders met in Niagara Falls, New York, in 1906 and launched the Niagara Movement to advance political and economic rights for blacks. They made clear their determination in this mission statement:

> We refuse to allow the impression to remain that the Negro-American assents to inferiority, is submissive under oppression and apologetic before insults. Through helplessness we may submit, but the voice of protest of ten million Americans must never cease to assail the ears of their fellow so long as America is unjust.[21]

A few years earlier, other African Americans had formed the National Afro-American Council and the National Organization of Colored Women. Both organizations fought against lynchings and other injustices. But Du Bois's crusade was all-encompassing. It was, in fact, the birth of the modern civil rights movement. In 1910 the Niagara Movement merged with a group of sympathetic whites. The new interracial union christened itself the National Association for the Advancement of Colored People (NAACP).

Soon, the NAACP's cadre of lawyers, investigators, educators, and publicists were waging a major civil rights crusade. The group's most urgent goal was to put an end to the lynchings that still plagued the South. Though such executions were clearly illegal, southern lawmen generally stood aside; investigation was rare, arrest even rarer. Thus, the NAACP lobbied hard to make lynching a federal crime that would be handled by outside federal investigators.

But white southerners used stalling techniques during debates in Congress to kill the proposal. Though NAACP members failed to get a federal lynching law, they did gain something important—the experience of working together toward a common goal. This training was soon put to the test when Jim Crow practices appeared in the federal government.

Jim Crow at the Federal Level

For decades the federal government had been one of the few major employers in the nation that did not discriminate against

President Wilson's Use of Jim Crow Questioned

In November 1913 a black delegation led by civil rights leader Monroe Trotter met Woodrow Wilson to protest his order to segregate the federal bureaucracy. This exchange between the two men is extracted from Eyewitness: A Living Documentary of the African American Contribution to American History, *edited by William Loren Katz.*

"[Mr. Monroe Trotter.] Mr. President, we are here to renew our protest against the segregation of colored [federal] employees. . . . We [had] appealed to you to undo this race segregation in accord with your duty as President and with your pre-election pledges to colored American voters. We stated that such segregation was a public humiliation and degradation, and entirely unmerited and far-reaching in its injurious effects. . . .

[President Woodrow Wilson.] The white people of the country, as well as I, wish to see the colored people progress, and admire the progress they have already made. . . . There is, however, a great prejudice against colored people. . . . It will take one hundred years to eradicate this prejudice, and we must deal with it as practical men. Segregation is not humiliating but a benefit, and ought to be so regarded by you gentlemen. If your organization goes out and tells the colored people of the country that it is a humiliation, they will so regard it, but if you do not tell them so, and regard it rather as a benefit, they will regard it the same. The only harm that will come will be if you cause them to think it is a humiliation.

[Mr. Trotter.] . . . [The facts do not support the claim that segregation was started because white and black federal clerks could not get along. It is clear] . . . that for fifty years white and colored clerks have been working together in peace and harmony and friendliness, doing so even through two Democratic administrations. Soon after your inauguration began, segregation was drastically introduced in the Treasury and Postal departments by your appointees.

[President Wilson.] If this organization is ever to have another hearing before me it must have another spokesman. Your manner offends me. . . . Your tone, with its background of passion.

[Mr. Trotter.] But I have no passion in me, Mr. President, you are entirely mistaken; you misinterpret my earnestness for passion."

blacks. But this policy suddenly changed in 1912 with the election of Democrat Woodrow Wilson. Blacks were shocked and angered when the new president issued an executive order that required all federal workplaces, restrooms, and cafeterias to be segregated.

Segregationist lawmakers were delighted by Wilson's action and promptly introduced bills designed to give it extra legal support. This time, the NAACP and other civil rights groups successfully pressured legislators to kill the bills; however, they were unable to undo Wilson's order.

The Impact of War

The outbreak of World War I in 1914 redirected the focus of civil rights groups and created new tensions between black and white Americans. When the United States entered the war in 1917, 360,000 black troops joined the fight, but did so in segregated units and encountered racism instead of gratitude for their sacrifices. Few black enlistees were given positions of responsibility and black officers were often treated contemptuously by white military commanders.

African Americans serving in France found a startling contrast in the French treatment of black people. French black soldiers served side by side with whites. They were not treated as inferiors. French society was not segregated. Blacks and whites freely mingled in cafés, restaurants, and stores.

Worried that American blacks might rebel against their segregated status, American military leaders asked the French to

An all-black regiment deployed in France during World War I. Although blacks fought in the war, they did so in segregated units and were seldom given the same level of responsibility as their white counterparts.

Discrimination on the Fields of War

The discrimination endured during World War II by Howard H. Long, an American officer, and other black soldiers is evident in this passage from Eyewitness: A Living Documentary of the African American Contribution to American History, *edited by William Loren Katz.*

"Many of the field officers seemed far more concerned with reminding their Negro subordinates that they were Negroes than they were with having an effective unit that would perform well in combat. There was extreme concern lest the Negro soldiers be on too friendly terms with the French people. An infamous order from division headquarters . . . made speaking to a French woman a disciplinary offense. . . .

We were billeted in Joneville, Haute Marne [France], for a period of training, where the men moved freely among the populace. For no obvious reason we were moved out on the drill ground a quarter of a mile away and even the officers were forbidden to return to the village. When the townspeople came out on the following Sunday they found that the Negro soldiers had been prohibited from meeting and talking with them. . . . One officer was put under arrest, guarded by a private with fixed bayonet, because the commanding officer saw him exchange a note with a French lady across the line."

avoid fraternizing with America's black soldiers. French officials obliged their ally's request with instructions to their officers such as the following:

> Although a citizen of the United States, the black man is regarded by the white American as an inferior being. . . . We must prevent the rise of any pronounced degree of intimacy between French officers, and black officers. . . . *We must not eat with [blacks], must not shake hands or seek to talk or meet with them outside of the requirements of military service.*[22]

Having fought for democracy overseas, many American black veterans returned home in 1918 determined to fight their own war for freedom in their native land. Proclaimed Du Bois in *Crisis*, the official publication of the NAACP, "Make way for Democracy! We saved it in France and by the great Jehovah, we will save it in the United States of America, or know the reason why."[23]

3 Black Attitudes Change

Blacks' changing attitudes toward accepting second-class treatment after World War I frightened many whites and rekindled old fears and prejudices. As a result, many white southerners vigorously opposed changing the status quo.

Prejudice against African Americans ran high in the North, too. Labor shortages during the war had given many southern blacks employment opportunities in northern factories. When World War I ended, racial strife developed as returning veterans competed for work.

Another legacy of the war in Europe took the form of a growing hostility in the United States toward all foreigners and alien ideas. Americans everywhere were suspicious of the communist revolution that had taken place in Russia, where revolutionaries promised to create a society based on equality for all people and advocated worldwide revolution. In the South this suspicion took on a unique racial twist. In his highly acclaimed book *The Mind of the South*, W. S. Cash observed that white southerners conjured up "yet another reason for fear and hate—the bogy of the Negro turning communist and staging a Red revolution in the South."[24]

Ready to halt a communist revolution and other imagined dangers was the newly reborn Ku Klux Klan, which reorganized in 1915 and began a campaign of terror against Catholics and Jews as well as blacks. This time the Klan spread far beyond the South. Local chapters appeared in Portland, Denver, Detroit, and other cities across the nation. Wherever the Klan appeared, it used kidnappings, cross burnings, beatings, and murder to terrorize its victims.

The collision of white paranoia and black assertiveness led to a burst of racial violence across the nation. Twenty-five race riots took place in Tulsa, Knoxville, Chicago, Washington, D.C., and other cities during the second half of 1919 alone. Lynch mobs hanged seventy blacks in the same year; ten of the victims were war veterans in uniform.

Even more horrible crimes occurred. Historian John Hope Franklin relates, "In 1921 a Negro was burned to death over a slow fire at Nodena, Arkansas. In the following year a mob, including women and children, slowly roasted a black man in Hubbard, Texas, while jabbing sticks into his mouth, nose, and eyes."[25]

Jim Crow Expands

As racial tension grew in the postwar years, segregationists expanded Jim Crow laws to

The Ku Klux Klan gained a resurgence following World War I. This 1925 photo shows Klan members marching toward the Washington Monument in a show of solidarity.

keep up with new technologies. This was especially true in the area of public transportation. Separate seating arrangements, for example, were imposed on taxi operators and cross-country buses in the South. Segregated waiting rooms, water fountains, and restrooms were installed at bus terminals, and at the new airports being built around the nation, black and white passengers were required to stay in separate waiting areas.

The increasing harshness of the Long Night caused blacks to leave the South in ever greater numbers. Any discrimination they faced in the North paled in comparison to the almost feudal existence imposed on them in the old Confederacy.

Black Migration Aids the Movement

This black migration eventually served as a catalyst for the unfolding civil rights movement. For one thing, blacks could, and did, vote in the North. As their political strength grew, a growing concentration of blacks in northern and midwestern cities also contributed to a greater sense of solidarity and power. African Americans were no longer confined to the comparatively backward mentality of the rural South. In the big northern cities, they were exposed to new ideas and had access to many powerful civil rights groups.

Population shifts also helped the NAACP grow. The number of its local chapters increased from fifty to more than five hundred during the two decades following the end of World War I. And as the organization grew, it stepped up its efforts to seek reforms through both the legislatures and courts of the nation.

The growing concentration of blacks in cities gave rise to another civil rights group, the Urban League, a social service organization founded in 1910 that concentrated on working with white employers to find good jobs for blacks.

The Impact of the Great Depression

The Great Depression of the 1930s resulted in a near total collapse of the American economy. African Americans, already at the bottom of the economic ladder, suffered the most.

But the Great Depression also proved to be a turning point in the struggle for civil rights. In 1932 the nation's new president, Franklin Delano Roosevelt (FDR), and his wife, Eleanor, quickly demonstrated a willingness to risk criticism from conservative whites to advance the cause of African Americans. FDR's political response to the Great Depression went a long way in boosting the spirits of many Americans, especially the poor. Scores of federally funded job programs and other

economic incentives became available to millions of citizens, black and white.

Eleanor Roosevelt was an outspoken supporter of black civil rights. In 1939 she publicly championed the cause of Marian Anderson, a celebrated opera singer whose scheduled recital at Constitution Hall in Washington, D.C., was canceled by the owners of the concert hall—the Daughters of the American Revolution— when they realized that Anderson was black. Infuriated, Mrs. Roosevelt arranged for the contralto to perform on the steps of the Lincoln Memorial before seventy-five thousand admirers. Anderson's courage and Mrs. Roosevelt's steadfast support gave the civil rights movement a needed boost.

Crowds of people wait in line for a hot meal during the Great Depression.

Eleanor Roosevelt presents the Springarn Medal of the NAACP to Marian Anderson in 1939. Roosevelt championed the cause of black civil rights throughout her life.

Until this time, most black Americans who retained the right to vote had remained loyal to the Republican Party. But now they started to switch to the party of FDR, the Democrats. African Americans understood that racists controlled the Democratic Party in the South, not the entire nation. Indeed, southern Democrats had kept a steely grip on southern society. But by early 1941, their grasp began to weaken when the United States once again prepared for war.

The Second World War

As another war loomed, thousands of new jobs in America's defense industries once again opened up. Blacks flocked to the in-dustrial centers in the North seeking the high-paying jobs. At first, however, most of the positions went to whites only. According to the U.S. Employment Service, of the eight thousand Americans who worked in aviation plants only thirteen were blacks.

Civil rights leaders were infuriated. A. Philip Randolph, a civil rights pioneer who served as president of the Brotherhood of Sleeping Car Porters labor union, threatened a massive black protest unless African Americans were given equal consideration in hiring.

Roosevelt, realizing a major protest march in the nation's capital would cause additional disruption during a tense time, issued Executive Order 8802, which stated:

> There shall be no discrimination in the employment of workers in defense industries or government because of race, creed, color, or national origin.

Civil rights leader and union organizer A. Philip Randolph protested the government's hiring practices during World War II.

Black troops train in the trenches in preparation for World War II. One million blacks served in segregated units in the U.S. armed forces during the war.

. . . It is the duty of employers and of labor organizations to provide for the full and equitable participation of all workers in defense industries, without discrimination.[26]

FDR's response satisfied Randolph; the march was called off. Though this order was not thoroughly enforced in the South, it opened up new economic opportunities for America's black workers and prompted many civil rights workers to declare Roosevelt's action a "second emancipation."

But a million black men who served in the armed forces during America's involvement in World War II (1941–1945) discovered Jim Crow practices were well in place.

With few exceptions, African Americans once again fought in segregated black units commanded by white officers and experienced racism at U.S. military bases everywhere.

And at the war's conclusion, black veterans could not help but contrast the Allied victory over the nondemocratic regimes of Germany, Italy, and Japan with the bitter fact that they were not totally free in their own country. Adding to their sense of insult was the fact that some American whites treated German prisoners with more dignity than they did the nation's black defenders: "No Negro who had seen it could ever erase from his mind the sight of . . . [German] war prisoners enjoying better treatment and more luxury than a Negro American could ever dream of enjoying in his own country,"[27] writes John Hope Franklin.

African Americans were also irked by the injustice of seeing Germans who immigrated to the United States after the war quickly absorbed into an American white society that simultaneously excluded African Americans.

Jim Crow Under International Scrutiny

The United States emerged from WWII as a world power and leading proponent of democracy. But soon it was locked in a dangerous struggle for power and prestige with the communist regime of the Soviet Union. Soviet leaders relished using tales of Jim Crow for its anti-American propaganda campaign. Many American officials suspected Soviet agents were exploiting the unhappiness of American blacks by trying to persuade them to revolt against the American system.

In 1946 the Committee on Civil Rights, appointed by President Harry Truman, revealed just how serious the federal government thought the problem was:

> We cannot escape the fact that our civil rights record has been an issue in world politics. . . . Those with competing philosophies have stressed—and are shamelessly distorting—our shortcomings. . . . They have tried to prove our democracy an empty fraud, and our nation a consistent oppressor of underprivileged people.[28]

World War II and Racial Justice

The National Experience: A History of the United States *includes an excerpt from A. Philip Randolph's 1942 keynote address to the policy conference of the March on Washington Movement that outlines his views on war and racial justice in America.*

"We know that our fate is tied up with the fate of the democratic way of life. And so, out of the depths of our hearts, a cry goes up for the triumph of the United Nations. But we would not be honest with ourselves were we to stop with a call for a victory of arms alone. . . . Unless this war sounds the death knell to the old Anglo-American empire systems, the hapless story of which is one of exploitation for the profit and power of a monopoly capitalist economy, it will have been fought in vain. Our aim then must not only be to defeat nazism, fascism, and militarism on the battlefield but to win the peace, for democracy, for freedom and the Brotherhood of Man without regard to his pigmentation, land of his birth or the God of his fathers."

A black man enters a theater through the "colored" entrance in this 1939 photograph.

The committee recommended several corrective measures. It suggested that the Department of Justice assume a greater role in prosecuting violations of civil rights. It recognized a need for a permanent federal Commission on Civil Rights. And it urged Congress to make lynching a federal crime and to outlaw voting discrimination and racial discrimination in the workplace.

Not since Reconstruction had the federal government shown such open concern for civil rights. Congress, however, failed to implement any of the committee's recommendations.

Truman took action on his own in 1948 by issuing a presidential order that desegregated the nation's armed forces. In addition he ordered the promotion of more black officers. Both decisions provoked a firestorm of controversy.

Meanwhile, several federal agencies quietly desegregated many jobs. These steps, however, helped only a relatively few American blacks. Across the nation, racial discrimination kept millions of other blacks powerless and poor.

Nonetheless, African Americans everywhere found themselves energized by the economic, social, and political winds of change brought on by WWII. Journalist John Gunther observed this phenomenon when he toured the nation at the end of the war: "The Negro community is probably more unified today, more politically vehement, more aggressive in its demand for full citizenship—even in the South—than in any other time in history."[29]

Invigorated by this new spirit of unity, the civil rights movement set out to end the Long Night. Its dark veils were soon to part.

Chapter

4 The Walls of Segregation Begin to Crack

Even before the end of World War II, civil rights organizations intensified their crusade to end Jim Crow. The Congress of Racial Equality (CORE), for instance, decided on peaceful protest. Founded on the principles of nonviolence of India's great leader, Mahatma Gandhi, CORE volunteers challenged segregation through passive resistance at restaurants, waiting rooms, and other areas.

Other black leaders, meanwhile, concentrated on lobbying efforts for new anti-discrimination laws. But this approach was almost an impossibility in the South, where all state legislatures were dominated by whites. Neither did Democrats nor Republicans at the federal level show much interest in promoting civil rights for African Americans.

To some civil rights activists, the best hope for African Americans lay in the nation's federal courts. Most federal judges were white men, but they were also highly educated individuals who had sworn to act impartially and to base their decisions on the nation's laws. Furthermore, they were obliged to uphold the constitutional guarantees of civil rights for all Americans.

And though these judges did not pass laws, they did have the power of judicial

Young volunteers work for the NAACP, an organization that encouraged blacks to use anti-discrimination laws already in place to fight for their civil rights.

review; that is, the power to determine whether certain laws were in violation of the principles expressed in the Constitution. The key to victory, according to many rights leaders, was to convince federal judges to strike down existing laws that discriminated against minorities.

Battling in the Courts

In fact, a handful of civil rights attorneys had already patiently chipped away at the wall of segregation in the nations' courts for years. In 1933, Nathan Ross Margold, a white lawyer for the NAACP, drafted a legal strategy he believed lawyers could use to end segregated schools across the nation. Known as the Margold Report, this document argued that the *Plessy* decision was weak because it depended too heavily on laws and judicial decisions that predated the Fourteenth Amendment.

The Margold Report remained a theoretical exercise, however, until Charles Houston, a respected African American law professor, took leave from Howard University in Washington, D.C., to become the chief counsel for the NAACP. Using the report as his guide, Houston set out to attack segregation in education. A victory here, he thought, would create a powerful precedent, or model case, that would establish the legal framework for dismantling the separate-but-equal doctrine based on *Plessy*.

Rather than first targeting public elementary or secondary schools, however, Houston decided to go after Jim Crow practices in graduate programs, in part because a case aimed at adult students would likely generate less white hostility than one

Law professor Charles Houston was instrumental in eliminating segregation in American colleges and universities.

involving young children whose protective parents might react more emotionally.

Houston also had another reason. Discrimination on the graduate level was blatant and difficult to defend legally. Southern states had a well-established dual public school system for black and white children. But since so few African Americans furthered their education past the undergraduate college level, most southern universities had no graduate programs for blacks. Most simply denied blacks entrance yet offered no segregated alternatives; equality of education, therefore, did not exist.

Thus, Houston believed a well-reasoned argument would compel segregationist states to take one of two remedial actions.

Either they would have to permit black students to attend all-white classes, or they would have to pay for their education at an out-of-state institution. But Houston believed that any states that did require a student to leave the state also violated the Fourteenth Amendment, which promised due process to all citizens.

Armed with this legal strategy and assisted by a rising young black lawyer named Thurgood Marshall, Houston prepared to do legal battle against the titans of Jim Crow.

Early Victories

Their first case was that of Donald G. Murray, an African American who was denied entrance to the University of Maryland's exclusively white law school. In June 1935, Houston and Marshall argued in a Baltimore municipal court that Murray was being deprived of a right to an education "equal" to that of the state's whites because there was no black law school. Moreover, they said, the state of Maryland had to fulfill its responsibility to educate one of its citizens.

The judge agreed and ordered the school to admit Murray. Suddenly, the NAACP had achieved a major victory. As a result, many southern states began to spend more money on their graduate and professional programs for blacks.

Another opportunity to challenge segregation came three years later when Lloyd Lionel Gaines, a twenty-five-year-old black man, was denied entrance to the all-white law school at the University of Missouri solely on the basis of his race. The state argued that Gaines would get an equal edu-

cation if it built a law school at its all-black Lincoln University. But construction could take years. If Gaines did not want to wait, Missouri would pay for his education at an out-of-state law school.

Instead, Gaines sued to be admitted to the white law school. Two and a half years went by as his case slowly worked its way through the appeals process before finally reaching the Supreme Court.

On December 12, 1938, the Supreme Court ruled in Gaines's favor. Once again the civil rights movement scored a powerful victory. Author Juan Williams explains the legal significance of the case:

> The Supreme Court opinion made it clear that states had an obligation to provide an equal education for their citizens, black and white; that they could not send black students out of the state instead of providing in-state facilities to educate them; and that they could not ask students to wait while they built those schools within the state.[30]

By the late 1940s civil rights lawyers were zeroing in on the *Plessy* decision. By now many believed *Plessy* was so legally flawed that the high court could be persuaded to overturn the decision. But they also knew that such a legal reversal was something the Supreme Court rarely did.

Two more cases paved the way for a showdown on *Plessy*. On June 5, 1950, the Supreme Court ruled in *Sweatt v. Painter* that a University of Texas law program set up in rented basements for blacks was not equal to the one it offered to whites.

On the same day, in *McLaurin v. Oklahoma*, the Court ruled against the segregationist practices of the University of Oklahoma. In this case, the university had admitted a black student, George McLaurin, to a graduate program for whites. But university officials required him to be isolated from the other students in classrooms, the school library, and the cafeteria. For example, in class McLaurin had to sit some distance from white students at a desk designated "reserved for colored." This treatment, the Court said, violated the Fourteenth Amendment's promise of equal treatment.

Though the Supreme Court had not overturned the *Plessy* decision, the outcomes of *Sweatt v. Painter* and *McLaurin v. Oklahoma* quickly caught the attention of officials in colleges and universities in the South. One school after another changed its policies regarding minorities. Explains C. Vann Woodward:

> And so for the first time, except for [a few instances after the Civil War] Negro students appeared with white students at Southern state institutions. By the fall of 1953 they were enrolled in twenty-three publicly supported colleges in Southern or border states at

the graduate level, and in ten at the undergraduate level. All this had been done without violence or serious resistance, but it was done on a token basis and before an uglier mood of defiance had developed.[31]

This spirit of compliance, however, had no effect on the vast majority of America's public elementary and secondary schools. This was especially true in the South, where segregation remained in full force. Most southern public schools, in fact, were segregated by law. As a result, approximately 11 million children in the South, the border states, and Washington, D.C., still attended racially segregated schools.

White segregationists were worried. They well understood that the federal courts were clearly whittling away the legal foundations of the separate-but-equal concept that had defined race relations for more than fifty years. Trying to head off any future court orders to desegregate, many southern communities tried to upgrade their local black schools to make them more equal to white schools. Finding

Thurgood Marshall (left) and Charles Houston (right) took on many civil rights cases, including the suit against the University of Maryland in 1935. In the decision that followed the case, the judge ordered the university to admit Donald G. Murray, a black man, into the school.

the extra funding for this undertaking was hard to do in the poorest region of the nation, but by 1952 most southern states were spending up to eight times as much on building and maintaining black schools as they had done a decade earlier.

Meanwhile, other legal challenges that had the potential to do away with school segregation forever were wending their way through the federal court system.

Brown v. Board of Education

What became one of the most important court cases in U.S. history originated not in the South, but in Topeka, Kansas—one of four western states that permitted local school boards to segregate their school systems. The landmark case centered on a seven-year-old girl, Linda Brown, who lived just five blocks away from a public elementary school. Local school authorities refused to let Brown attend this school because she was black. Instead, she was told to enroll in a school for blacks located twenty-one blocks away.

Linda Brown's parents were incensed. They considered the school for blacks not only inconvenient but also inferior to the nearby white school. And when school officials refused to rescind their decision, Linda's father, Oliver Brown, filed a lawsuit to challenge the school board's policy.

The NAACP took up Brown's case and its legal counsel decided on a new legal attack. As Hugh Speer, a professor at the University of Missouri and expert witness for the NAACP, explains:

> The day before the trial, the lawyers and several witnesses agreed to [argue] that the building and books [in black schools] were inferior as a strategy to divert the defense lawyer . . . but to put the emphasis on the social and psychological damage of segregation . . . regardless of whether . . . the facilities were comparable. This strategy marked a distinct turning point in the history of segregation cases.[32]

During the trial, Louisa Holt Howe, a social psychologist at the Menninger Foundation Clinic in Topeka, pointed out:

Linda Brown in 1964, ten years after her parents petitioned the courts to allow her to attend her neighborhood school in Topeka, Kansas.

Plaintiffs from Prince Edward County, Virginia, assemble on the steps of Virginia's capitol building during the trial of Brown v. Board of Education.

The fact that [segregation] is enforced, that it is legal, I think, has more importance than the fact of segregation itself because this gives legal and official sanction to a policy which is inevitably interpreted by both black and white people as denoting the inferiority of the Negro group.[33]

Despite this and similar testimony from six other social scientists on behalf of Linda Brown, the Topeka court ruled unanimously for the defendant. Its main reason for doing so, explained the presiding judge, was that "separate but equal" was still the law of the land. A decision to reverse this legal standard was up to the Supreme Court.

Brown was not the only case of its kind; four related lawsuits had been filed in South Carolina, Delaware, Virginia, and Washington. When these cases reached the Supreme Court along with *Brown*, they were consolidated into a single case designated as *Oliver Brown v. Board of Education of Topeka, Kansas.*

After hearing lengthy arguments from both sides, the Supreme Court took a year to consider its verdict. Finally, on the morning of May 17, 1954, Chief Justice Earl Warren announced the Court's unanimous ruling:

We come then to the question presented: Does segregation of children in public schools solely on the basis of race, even though the physical facilities and other "tangible" factors may be equal, deprive the children of the minority group of equal educational opportunities? We believe that it does. . . . To separate [children] from others of similar age and qualifications solely because of their race generates a feeling of inferiority as to their status in the community that may affect their heart and minds in a way unlikely ever to be undone. . . .

We conclude that in the field of public education the doctrine of "separate but equal" has no place. Separate educational facilities are inherently unequal.[34]

The decision was a legal blockbuster. Fifty-eight years after *Plessy v. Ferguson*, the Supreme Court had reversed itself, at least as far as public education was concerned. By eradicating "separate but equal" as a legal concept, the Court had delivered a decisive blow to the legal foundation of segregation.

Black Americans rejoiced everywhere. Astonishingly, they found themselves backed, not blocked, by the nation's courts. Civil rights leaders, however, had no illusions that the Supreme Court's decision had made their struggle easy. Much hard work to improve the education of black children remained to be done. Still, many took satisfaction in knowing that their hard work had at last toppled one of the legal pillars of segregation.

But other pillars remained. Jim Crow laws and practices set up to impose second-class citizenship status on African Americans still existed in the South. This fact soon became clear in Montgomery, Alabama, one of the most segregated cities in the nation.

The Montgomery Bus Boycott

Within days of the *Brown* decision, Jo Ann Robinson, the president of the Women's Political Council in Montgomery, sent a letter to the city's mayor that protested mistreatment of blacks on the city's buses.

Though whites and blacks rode the same buses together, blacks were required to obey demeaning Jim Crow laws. They were forced to enter the bus from the rear and sit in a designated "colored" section. Whenever there were not enough seats in the white section, black passengers were expected to give up their places to whites. Any black who failed to do so could be arrested and jailed. In Selma, Alabama, black passengers had even been killed for not observing the bus policy.

Now in the exciting aftermath of the Supreme Court's momentous decision, Jo Ann Robinson set out to end an unjust system in her community. She warned the mayor that since the majority of bus riders were blacks, they had the power to shut down the bus system by refusing to ride it.

The mayor ignored Robinson's complaint, but the issue did not go away. All that was needed for a citywide confrontation was a single spark. And that flash point came on December 1, 1955, when a Montgomery resident, Mrs. Rosa Parks, boarded a city bus. Having worked all day as a seamstress in a downtown store, she was tired and sat down on a bus seat to rest. Several stops later, the bus driver ordered Parks and other blacks to give their seats to whites standing in the aisle. Three black passengers did as they were told. Parks refused. The indignant bus driver promptly called the police, who sent an officer to arrest Parks and take her to jail.

News of Rosa Parks's arrest flashed through Montgomery's black community. That night forty prominent blacks met to discuss the matter. Among those attending were Jo Ann Robinson, a seasoned NAACP worker named E. D. Dixon, and the Reverend Ralph Abernathy, a stocky minister of the First Baptist Church.

Also present was a newcomer to Montgomery, the Reverend Dr. Martin Luther King Jr., the handsome, scholarly minister of Dexter Avenue Baptist Church. King was only twenty-six years old, but fellow blacks quickly recognized his abilities. Highly educated and intelligent, he displayed a considerable skill at oratory and powerful personal charisma.

During the meeting, the group formally organized itself into the Montgomery Improvement Association (MIA). "Although I felt the people in Montgomery had respect for me, I knew that a mass movement of 50,000 people required young, vigorous and well-educated leadership," Dixon later recalled. "I believed that if Rev. King and Rev. Abernathy could take over leadership of an improvement association, we could not fail."[35]

King and Abernathy assumed leadership with dozens of other local black leaders assisting. The MIA's immediate goal was to launch a massive protest against Rosa Parks's arrest by staging a one-day boycott

A Call To Action

The text of Jo Ann Robinson's mimeographed leaflets that sparked the Montgomery bus boycott appear in her memoir, The Montgomery Bus Boycott and the Women Who Started It.

"Another Negro woman has been arrested and thrown in jail because she refused to get up out of her seat on the bus for a white person to sit down. It is the second time since the Claudette Cloven case that a Negro woman has been arrested for the same thing. This has to be stopped. Negroes have rights, too, for if Negroes did not ride the buses, they could not operate. Three-fourths of the riders are Negroes, yet we are arrested, or have to stand over empty seats. If we do not do something to stop these arrests, they will continue.

The next time it may be you, or your daughter, or mother. This woman's case will come up on Monday. We are, therefore, asking every Negro to stay off the buses Monday in protest of the arrest and trial. Don't ride the buses to work, to town, or school, or anywhere on Monday. You can afford to stay out of school for one day if you have no other way to go except by bus. You can also afford to stay out of town for one day. If you work, take a cab, or walk. But please, children and grown-ups, don't ride the bus at all on Monday. Please stay off of all buses Monday."

of the city buses. Later that night, Jo Ann Robinson and a few other volunteers printed up flyers that urged fellow black citizens of Montgomery—who made up 75 percent of Montgomery's bus riders—to stay off the buses.

Early the next Monday, the city buses rolled as usual—but most of Montgomery's fifteen thousand black bus riders were not aboard. Instead, many formed carpools to get to work. Some walked. Others rode mules. King remembered:

> All day long it continued. . . . During the rush hours the sidewalks were crowded with laborers and domestic workers, . . . trudging patiently to their jobs and home again, sometimes as much as twelve miles. They knew why they walked, and the knowledge was evident in the way they carried themselves. And as I watched them I knew that there is nothing more majestic than the determined courage of individuals willing to suffer and sacrifice for their freedom and dignity.[36]

That night boycott supporters gathered at Montgomery's Holt Street Baptist Church to discuss the day's event. Among the speakers was King, who recounted the details of Rosa Parks's arrest and went over the sad history of other abusive treatment of blacks on Montgomery buses. Then King added:

The Woman Who Started a Revolt

Rosa L. Parks, whose refusal to give up her bus seat to a white person ignited the Montgomery bus boycott, recalls what happened when two policemen arrived to investigate the complaint against her in this passage selected from Documentary History of the Modern Civil Rights Movement, *edited by Peter B. Levy.*

"They approached me and asked if the driver had asked me to stand up, and I said yes, and they wanted to know why I didn't. I told them I didn't think I should have to stand up. After I had paid my fare and occupied a seat, I didn't think I should have to give it up.

They placed me under arrest then and had me get in the police car, and I was taken to jail and booked on suspicion, I believe. The questions were asked, the usual questions they ask a prisoner or somebody under arrest. They had to determine whether the driver wanted to press charges or swear out a warrant, which he did. Then they took me to jail and I was placed in a cell. In a little while I was taken from the cell, and my picture was made and fingerprints taken. I went back to the cell then, and a few minutes later I was called back again, and when this happened I found out that Mr. E. D. Dixon and Mrs. Clifford Durr had come to make bond for me."

Rosa Parks is fingerprinted after her arrest for not giving up her seat on a public bus to a white person.

cans were beaten. Boycott leaders received death threats. King's home was bombed, though he and his wife and child were unhurt. Another bomb damaged the home of E. D. Nixon. Outraged by the acts of violence, many blacks took to the streets, brandishing guns and threatening revenge. But time and time again King counseled his followers not to respond to violence with violence. Like the members of CORE, he adhered to Gandhi's principle of passive resistance, and he was faithful to the Christian teachings of nonviolence. But King had also read "Civil Disobedience" by nineteenth-century American writer Henry David Thoreau, which

The Reverend Martin Luther King Jr., perhaps the most articulate spokesman for black civil rights.

But there comes a time that people get tired. We are here this evening to say to those who have mistreated us so long that we are tired—tired of being segregated and humiliated; tired of being kicked about by the brutal feet of oppression. We had no alternative but to protest.[37]

The one-day boycott worked so well that MIA leaders decided to extend it until Montgomery's white leaders agreed to change the bus policy and let blacks sit wherever they wanted. They also insisted that the city's bus drivers treat black riders politely.

When Montgomery's white leadership refused these demands, a battle of nerves began. For the next 381 days, African Americans continued their boycott. Racial tension mounted as groups of angry whites tried to frighten and harass blacks into backing down. Some African Ameri-

Rev. Ralph Abernathy (left, foreground) leads a meeting of those who organized the bus boycott in Montgomery, Alabama.

emphasized the moral necessity of disobeying unjust laws. And Montgomery's segregated bus-seating policy, thought King, was anything but just.

The boycott hurt many people financially. The bus company lost money. White merchants who depended on black patronage also suffered. In fact, unable to tolerate a prolonged slide in revenues, many white downtown merchants pressured city officials to agree to the boycotters' demands.

Montgomery's white power structure stubbornly refused to capitulate. At one point, city authorities became so frustrated that they had King and eighty-nine other MIA members arrested on trumped-up charges of conspiring to destroy the bus company. On the day of his trial, King was found guilty and fined five hundred dollars.

Such tactics, however, failed to stop the young minister and his fellow civil rights workers. As the boycott continued, the MIA unleashed another action. With legal assistance from the NAACP, it filed lawsuits challenging Montgomery's bus segregation policies.

The legal attack proved successful a year later when the Supreme Court outlawed Montgomery's discriminatory bus laws. The Court's decision meant the Montgomery boycotters could now ride the bus and sit anywhere they wanted, just like any other American citizen.

Remembers Virginia Durr, a Montgomery white who sympathized with the boycotters, "When I heard that the boycott had been successful, I felt pure, unadulterated joy. . . . Of course, the blacks felt that way, but the white friends I had felt the way I did. We felt joy and release. It was as if a great burden had fallen off us."[38]

But the MIA's triumph was not merely a local one. The boycotters had demonstrated that African Americans could band together to fight nonviolently for a just cause, and win. They also proved that highly reasoned principles and uncommon leadership could triumph in the face of violence and bigotry. Electrified by the example in Montgomery, blacks across the South launched their own crusades against local Jim Crow laws and practices.

The victory in Montgomery had brought on yet another change. No longer was Martin Luther King simply the spokesman for a local civil rights campaign. His eloquence, leadership, and expert handling of the bus boycott had thrust him into the national arena. The growing civil rights movement now had a new and powerful leader.

The Rise of Martin Luther King

King soon became a well-known figure across the United States—and a controversial one. White segregationists regarded him as a brash troublemaker who stirred up racial discord. But to millions of other Americans, both white and black, the young Baptist preacher was an inspiration. Many considered him to be the most

Rosa Parks Reflects

In her book Quiet Strength, *Rosa Parks offers these ideas on civil rights nearly forty years after her act of quiet defiance on a Montgomery bus sparked an ever larger protest.*

"One thing we need to do is tell young people about our struggles for civil rights. I think they sometimes have difficulty separating fact from fiction when it comes to our history. It's important that they hear how things were and what some of us had to go through before them. Many of them do not appreciate the suffering their ancestors have endured to bring them the degree of freedom they now enjoy. They must be reminded that many people have died so that they can have what they have now.

Racism is still alive and will stay with us as long as we allow it. But we can teach our youth to continue the effort and not lose the gains we have achieved. We can show them how opportunities come along and how individuals today can still bring about change."

Martin Luther King Jr. addresses followers after an aborted march in Selma, Alabama. King's persistent call for the use of nonviolent tactics to fight discrimination influenced the entire civil rights movement.

important voice in the growing civil rights movement itself. Millions around the world were moved by his eloquent call for justice for America's blacks.

Suddenly, King was in demand as a public speaker. Groups everywhere wanted to hear him, especially small groups of black civil rights workers across the South who wanted his advice on how to launch their own crusades against Jim Crow.

Over and over, King told rapt audiences how the Montgomery boycotters had tried to conduct themselves peaceably. He also reminded his audiences that injustice—not white people—had been the group's adversary. As a Christian minister, King stressed the importance of spirituality in the crusade for equality.

In 1957 several black clergymen formed the Southern Christian Leadership Conference (SCLC), a national civil rights or-

ganization, in Atlanta's Ebenezer Baptist Church. King became its first president. One of the core beliefs of the new organization was the Christian precept that the souls of all humans could be rescued by the forgiveness of God. Thus, SCLC set out to "redeem the soul of America." With this principle in mind, the civil rights group meant to reform American society, not tear it down.

"Because we believed in this nation, we sought to remove the barriers that separated us from white society—not out of a need to be close to white people, but to gain the same access to society's benefits that they enjoyed,"[39] recalls Andrew Young, then a clergyman turned activist.

But as the SCLC grew in strength so did a formidable opposition of white segregationists across the South. Their response to the growing call to end segregation was "Never."

5 The Rise of White Militant Resistance

The Supreme Court decisions, the Montgomery bus boycott, and other civil rights actions in the early 1950s triggered a powerful white militant backlash. At the core of this reaction were diehard segregationists—Southern white politicians, community leaders, middle-class merchants, businesspeople, clergymen, and Klansmen—who opposed the activism of the federal government and the rising civil rights movement.

Major protests did not develop quickly, however. During the first year after the *Brown* decision, in fact, segregationists put up little organized resistance. But most southern school districts did little to comply with the Court's decision. For one thing, the Court had not said when or how schools must start integrating white and black students. Without any specific instructions to guide them, southern school boards moved slowly, or not at all, to desegregate on their own.

A year after the *Brown* ruling, on May 31, 1955, the Supreme Court handed down another decision instructing lower federal courts to make sure that local school districts desegregated "with all deliberate speed."

Many school systems in the border states between the North and South complied with the Court's order. In addition, forty private colleges and universities desegregated without conflict or any government coercion. Nurses, attorneys, social workers, and other professionals also opened up their professions to blacks. But these generally peaceful acts of integration were overshadowed by a larger backlash of anger and violence that accelerated after the second *Brown* ruling.

A Smoldering Hate

The resistance was especially strong in states of the Deep South, such as Alabama and Mississippi. Here a majority of whites still clung to a belief in white supremacy coupled with a deep mistrust, if not hatred, of the federal government. Most white southerners staunchly favored states' rights over those of the federal government, just as their forefathers had almost a century before during the Civil War. Many resented a distant governmental power that dictated racial policies affecting their daily lives. So strong was the southern faith in states' rights, in fact, that many political leaders publicly advanced the argument that states had the right to "nullify" any federal mandates that they found unacceptable.

Two girls—one black, the other white—look at each other from across their desks in 1954, shortly after the school in Fort Myer, Virginia, was integrated.

"On May 17, 1954, the Constitution of the United States was destroyed because of the Supreme Court's decision," Mississippi senator James Eastland told his fellow southerners. "You are not obliged to obey the decisions of any court which are plainly fraudulent [and based on] sociological considerations."[40]

Fear also fed the fury of whites. Many white parents were frightened by the prospect of their children socializing with blacks at school. Daily contact, they believed, could lead to interracial dating, marriage, and sexual relations. Such practices were both taboo and illegal throughout the South.

The Supreme Court's desegregation order also rekindled the old fear of black rebellion. Such a prospect especially terrified whites in many Mississippi counties who were vastly outnumbered by blacks.

They believed that equality with blacks at school would be the first step in a dangerous march towards black dominance and control.

Unvarnished racism contributed to the white counterrevolt as well. White supremacy groups counted among their members many who hated blacks and resented any attempt to elevate them to the status of whites. And these racists steeled themselves not only to resist, but also to destroy any threat to the current social order.

Outside Agitators?

Many whites refused to accept that their African American neighbors desired integration. They argued that the civil rights movement did not arise from southern blacks at all. Rather, it was all the work of outside agitators, radicals who had infiltrated the South only to upset the social order. Whites often charged that many civil rights workers were really communist infiltrators who stirred up the local black communities.

And though American communists played at best only a minor role in the civil rights movement, they had been visible enough in the past to provoke white anxiety. In 1929, for example, the American Communist Party took an active part in a major textile strike in Tennessee and the Carolinas that left southerners traumatized for decades.

In 1932, during the Great Depression, Angelo Herndon, a southern black nineteen-year-old, was one of several blacks who joined the Communist Party. He later explained why:

All my life I'd been sweated and stepped-on and Jim-Crowed. . . . I heard myself called "nigger" and "darky" and I had to say "Yes, sir" to every white man, whether he had my respect or not. . . . And here, all of a sudden, I had found organizations in which Negroes and whites sat together, and worked together, and knew no difference of race or color.[41]

Whites protest the integration of their junior high school in Little Rock, Arkansas. As blacks gained ground, average whites fought for things to remain the same.

In the ultraconservative South, any talk of racial equality was generally viewed as treason by segregationists. Herndon, in fact, was arrested and convicted in Atlanta on charges of leading an insurrection after he led a protest march in support of welfare for the unemployed. Herndon later recalled the racist tenor of the prosecutor's questions during the trial:

> Did I believe that . . . Negroes should have complete equality with white people? Did I believe in the demand for the self-determination of the Black Belt—that the Negro people should be allowed to rule the Black Belt territory, kicking out the white landlords and government officials?[42]

By the 1950s, conformity was the norm and suspicion of outsiders again swept the nation. Many Americans became convinced that the Soviet Union menaced the security of the United States. With its brutal dictatorship and zeal for world dominance, Soviet communists seemed to offer oppressed minorities everywhere promises of social and economic equality. Suspicion of communist infiltration dovetailed with the repugnance so many southern whites held for the civil rights movement and helped to fuel the fires of white rage following the two *Brown* decisions. And this backlash escalated when southerners saw how the desegregation order of the Supreme Court was being implemented.

Forcing Compliance

Buoyed by the fact that they had federal law on their side, civil rights workers took legal action against stubborn school boards to comply with the Supreme Court's decision. During the summer of 1955, the NAACP sued 170 local school boards in seventeen states to desegregate public schools.

But since the Supreme Court had left the details of implementing school desegregation plans in the hands of district judges, many white southerners at first thought they had little to fear concerning

Thurgood Marshall and the NAACP legal team at work. One by one, the NAACP took on schools that resisted the Supreme Court decision to desegregate schools.

desegregation. They were sure the judges—most of whom were native southerners—would find ways to interpret the ruling to the liking of segregationists.

Their faith was misplaced: Instead of obstructing the Supreme Court's order, most southern judges dutifully carried out their mandate from the Supreme Court by systematically overturning local school segregation laws across the South.

These unexpected judicial decisions, combined with a new assertiveness from civil rights organizations—especially the NAACP—appalled and frightened white segregationists. In response, many Southern leaders openly declared their disdain and vowed to fight all desegregation efforts. Senator Harry F. Byrd of Virginia implored whites everywhere to use "massive resistance" to block implementation of the *Brown* decision. On March 12, 1956, one hundred Southern congressmen signed *A Southern Manifesto*, which declared their unified opposition to integration. "Although the sentiment of the manifesto was not new, the document was significant because it put elected officials on record in opposition to *Brown*, and, arguably, legitimated other forms of resistance,"[43] observes Peter Levy.

State lawmakers responded enthusiastically. One by one, state governments of the old Confederacy passed two hundred new segregation laws. The sole purpose of many of these pieces of legislation was to give school districts ways to thwart desegregation. Mississippi, for instance, amended its constitution to allow local school districts to abolish public schools. Virginia's Prince Edward County school system closed its schools rather than comply. And Georgia lawmakers made it a felony to spend taxpayers' money on integrated schools. Some southern school districts were allowed to use public money to fund "private schools"—that is, whites-only schools. Though virtually none of these laws would survive legal challenges, they did enable southern whites to stall the implementation process.

Southerners also had another weapon in their arsenal of delaying tactics, one made possible by the language used in the May 1955 implementation ruling:

> Full implementation of these constitutional principles may require solution of varied local school problems. School authorities have the primary responsibility for elucidating, assessing, and solving these problems.[44]

Essentially, the same school boards that opposed desegregation in the first place were empowered to implement the Court's order in whatever way they saw fit, which usually meant indefinite postponement. One of the most common delaying tactics involved state governments giving numerous local school officials the authority to make decisions about what schools children should attend. This fragmentation of decision making forced civil rights lawyers to spend extra time and money filing separate lawsuits against numerous individual authorities.

Southern legislators also used their lawmaking powers to wage war on their number-one enemy, the NAACP.

The Drive to Destroy the NAACP

Historian Aldon D. Morris explains how southern lawmakers launched their assault:

Special sessions of the state legislatures were called, and plans to destroy the organization were formulated. In most Southern states it was decided that the NAACP should be forced to make available its membership lists. Charges that NAACP was communistic or subversive were used to justify this demand.[45]

But the real reason for such legislation was clear to whites and blacks alike: White segregationists wanted membership lists so they could intimidate NAACP members with economic reprisals and violence. NAACP officials who refused to turn over these names were jailed. Refusal also gave white district attorneys an opportunity to obtain court injunctions to stop the organization from functioning. Alabama managed to close the NAACP down for nine years this way; for brief periods Texas and Louisiana did likewise.

This unified attack hurt the NAACP. Between 1955 and 1958, the organization lost 246 branches in the South. Overall membership also declined, and NAACP resources were diverted to costly legal battles to counter these attacks. But this downward trend slowed in 1958, when the Supreme Court ruled that Alabama's effort to force the NAACP to hand over its membership lists was unconstitutional.

Southern governments did not wage war on the NAACP alone. They were also joined by privately run white organizations that were determined to wreck the civil rights movement.

White Councils

The most powerful of the private groups were the "white councils" that first appeared

Klan members and their families gather in an initiation ceremony in 1956. The young girl in the foreground is one of the members to be initiated.

in Mississippi on July 11, 1954, and then spread to Louisiana, Texas, Arkansas, Georgia, and Florida. Claiming a half million members, these councils vowed to fight integration at all costs. "The Citizens' Council is the South's answer to the mongrelizers [abusive term for civil rights activists]," proclaimed a pamphlet put out by the Association of Citizens' Councils. "*We will not be integrated!* We are proud of our white blood and our white heritage of sixty centuries."[46]

The white councils tended to aim economic reprisals at anyone—black or white—

who helped desegregate schools. But more extreme hate groups, such as the Ku Klux Klan, the White Christians, and the Christian Civil League, were quick to use violence to express their rage.

And white rage did slow the progress of the civil rights movement in many places. In Belzoni, Mississippi, for instance, blacks who wanted to vote found their car windshields smashed. Vandals also plundered a black entertainment club and posted a note that read: "This is what will happen to Negroes who try to vote."[47]

In 1955 two NAACP organizers, Reverend George Lee and Lamar Smith, were murdered in Mississippi. And Emmett Till, a fourteen-year-old black Chicago boy visiting relatives in Sumner, Mississippi, paid a terrible price for saying "Bye, baby," to a pretty white woman in a country store. Days later his mangled, decomposing body was pulled from the Tallahatchie River. Wedged into his battered skull was a spent bullet.

The young boy's brutal murder shocked the nation. Racial tensions escalated when an all-white jury acquitted two white men—Roy Bryant and his half-brother, J. W. Milam—of Till's murder. Later, the men confessed their guilt when a journalist paid them $4,000 to tell their story. "Well, what else could I do?" Milam told the reporter. "He thought he was as good as any white man."[48]

By the late 1950s, white resistance had become so intense across the South that even moderate politicians sided with segregationists to stay in office. Several newspaper editors scaled back their criticism of the ongoing lynchings, beatings, book bannings, and harassment of intellectuals who spoke out against white terror. Even many whites who believed in the black cause now ruefully concluded that to keep order in their communities, authorities had to bully, intimidate, and terrorize those who aggressively pushed for an end to segregation.

Accused of murdering a fourteen-year-old black boy, Roy Bryant (left) and J. W. Milam (center) await the start of their trial. The all-white jury would later acquit the two half-brothers.

The severity of white bigotry became painfully clear to the nation and the entire world during an ugly confrontation at Little Rock High School.

Showdown in Little Rock

The public school system in Little Rock, Arkansas, like most other school systems in the South, had been slow to comply with the federal mandate to desegregate. But finally the school board came up with an integration plan that was both gradual and limited. The first phase of the plan called for enrollment of black students at the city's all-white Central High School in September 1957, with further integration of other area schools to follow.

Local white resistance soon surfaced. Worried parents of white children publicly expressed their anxieties over the possibility of race mixing at school social functions. They were reassured when Arkansas governor Orville Faubus publicly voiced his own opposition. Fearing that the school board's plan was in danger of being derailed, the Little Rock chapter of the NAACP filed suit in federal court seeking an order to force the school district to integrate its schools immediately. This legal action offended many whites who thought the school board was faithfully and diligently working toward a mixed school system. On April 27, 1957, an appellate court in St. Louis agreed that the school system was complying "with all deliberate speed."

In retaliation for the NAACP's lawsuit, white state lawmakers passed four separate prosegregation bills. One of these measures made attendance at integrated schools voluntary. Another required that

any organization that challenged the authority of a state official must provide detailed financial statements to a state agency. The intent of this law was clearly meant to sidestep and bog down the NAACP.

That summer racial tension in Little Rock was at an all-time high. Seventy-five black students were expected to enroll at Central High, but when summer vacation ended only nine were willing to attend. On August 27, at the urging of Governor Faubus, a hastily formed segregationist group, the Mothers' League of Little Rock Central High, went to court seeking an injunction to stop the integration effort on the grounds that it was necessary to prevent racial violence on campus. Governor Faubus himself took the stand and testified that law enforcement officers had confiscated guns and knives from students who planned to take them to school on opening day. Though the governor had no evidence for this claim, the presiding judge issued a temporary injunction that stopped the mixing of black and white students—for the moment.

Wiley Branton and Thurgood Marshall of the NAACP took the next step. On August 30 they went to the federal district court and asked that the injunction be lifted on the grounds that no evidence of violence existed. Judge Ronald N. Davies agreed. The school's integration plan, he said, should proceed.

But Governor Faubus responded to this tug-of-war in an unexpected manner. On September 2, just two days before the first day of school at Central High, he appeared on statewide television and announced that he had ordered Arkansas National Guard troops to surround Central High to block the nine students from entering the campus. This action was nec-

The Arkansas National Guard surrounds Central High to prevent integration in Little Rock, Arkansas. On September 4, 1957, the nine black students who were to attend the school had to face down troops as well as angry white protesters.

essary, he said, to "maintain or restore order and to protect the lives and property of citizens. . . . [Therefore, the schools] in Pulaski County, for the time being, must be operated on the same [segregated] basis as they have been operated in the past."[49] Otherwise, Faubus told the people of Arkansas, "Blood will run in the streets."[50]

In the wake of the governor's action, the school board's first response was to request "that no Negro student attempt to attend Central or any white high school until this dilemma is legally resolved."[51] But Judge Davies quickly resolved the impasse. Admit the black students, he ordered the school board. The board complied, but it requested that the parents of the nine students not accompany their children on opening day, September 4, on the grounds

that their presence might provoke mob action among the whites.

Thus, on the morning of September 4, nine black high school students arrived at Central High and found a huge, angry crowd of whites waiting for them. Whites shrieked, cursed, and spit on the young blacks as they made their way to the school entrance. The school superintendent had assured the students they would be protected this morning. But when Elizabeth Eckford, one of the nine black students, made her way through a howling din of hate to a guard posted in front of the school, she found that "He just looked straight ahead and didn't move to let me pass. I didn't know what to do. . . . When I tried to squeeze past him, he raised his bayonet, and then the other guards moved and raised their bayonets. . . . Somebody started yelling, '*Lynch her! Lynch her!*'"[52] Though Eckford was protected by two whites in the crowd and escorted to safety, the incident would haunt her for years.

None of the black students managed to enter the high school that day. And for the next seven days, Faubus kept the troops in place and refused to change his order.

Meanwhile, around the nation many Americans, shocked at the events in Little Rock, wondered if the president of the United States would take action against the governor for obstructing a federal court order.

On September 9, the Justice Department finished a review of the events in Little Rock and concluded that Faubus had no right to block the students. It filed a complaint with the federal district court and convinced Judge Davies to grant an injunction forcing the Arkansas governor to call off the troops.

On September 23, the nine beleaguered students finally entered the school, this time under a police escort. Curses, threats, and taunts from some white students greeted them inside the school. But more troubling was the menacing mob of adults that had gathered outside the school. Not even local police could disperse it. White thugs chased and beat a group of black journalists covering the event, mistakenly identified as the parents of the nine students. The mob also turned its wrath on nearby white journalists.

The black students did not stay very long at the school. Within hours, both school and police authorities grew fearful for the safety of the students and took

White high school students shout insults at Elizabeth Eckford as she attempts to go to school at Little Rock's Central High.

A Day of High School Terror

This passage from Eyewitness: A Living Documentary of the African American Contribution to American History is Elizabeth Eckford's account of the morning she left for Central High School in Little Rock, Arkansas, prepared to be one of nine students to cross the school's color line.

"Before I left home Mother called us into the living-room. She said we should have a word of prayer. Then I caught the bus and got off a block from the school. I saw a large crowd of people standing across the street from the soldiers guarding Central. As I walked on, the crowd suddenly got very quiet. Superintendent Blossom had told us to enter by the front door. I looked at all the people and thought, 'Maybe I will be safer if I walk down the block to the front entrance behind the guards.'

At the corner I tried to pass through the long line of guards around the school so as to enter the grounds behind them. One of the guards pointed across the street. So I pointed in the same direction and asked whether he meant for me to cross the street and walk down. He nodded 'yes.' So, I walked across the street conscious of the crowd that stood there, but they moved away from me.

For a moment all I could hear was the shuffling of their feet. Then someone shouted, 'Here she comes, get ready!' I moved away from the crowd on the sidewalk and into the street. If the mob came at me, I could then cross back over so the guards could protect me.

The crowd moved in closer and then began to follow me, calling me names. I still wasn't afraid. Just a little bit nervous. Then my knees started to shake all of a sudden and I wondered whether I could make it to the center entrance a block away. It was the longest block I ever walked in my whole life."

them home. This apprehension intensified when an even larger mob reappeared outside the school the next day.

By now Little Rock mayor Woodrow Mann was convinced his police force was not strong enough to maintain law and order outside the school. Mann called the Justice Department for help.

During this crisis, President Dwight Eisenhower had been reluctant to take any action in Little Rock. He argued that forcing the two races together would only result in conflict, bitterness, and resentment.

But Faubus's contempt for the law was now so flagrant and the danger of mob violence so imminent that the president at long last took action. On September 24, he ordered one thousand U.S. Army paratroopers to Little Rock to protect the nine students. In addition, he placed Arkansas's ten thousand National Guardsmen under his control, not the governor's.

The next day, federal troops escorted the frightened black teenagers to school. In addition, each student was assigned a personal bodyguard. Armed federal troops guarded the school hallways to protect the students and keep the peace for the next nine months.

All these turbulent events were recorded by TV cameras and beamed to the world. Many Americans were appalled by the violence, rancor, and ugliness in Little Rock. However, some questioned the wis-

White Political Leaders Take Their Stand

This sampling of "The Southern Manifesto: Declaration of Constitutional Principles" is taken from History of the Modern Civil Rights Movement, *edited by Peter B. Levy.*

"The unwarranted decision of the Supreme Court in the public school cases is now bearing the fruit always produced when men substitute naked power for established law. . . .

We regard the decision of the Supreme Court in the school cases as a clear abuse of judicial power. . . .

This unwarranted exercise of power by the Court, contrary to the Constitution, is creating chaos and confusion in the States principally affected. It is destroying the amicable [friendly] relations between the white and Negro races that have been created through 90 years of patient effort by the good people of both races. It has planted hatred and suspicion where there has been heretofore friendship and understanding.

Without regard to the consent of the governed, outside agitators are threatening immediate and revolutionary changes in our public-school systems. If done, this is certain to destroy the system of public education in some of the States.

With the gravest concern for the explosive and dangerous condition created by this decision and inflamed by outside meddlers. . . .

We pledge ourselves to use all lawful means to bring about a reversal of this decision which is contrary to the Constitution and to prevent the use of force in its implementation."

One of the nine black students to enter Central High is escorted by federal troops.

dom of armed intervention in public schools. Was integration perhaps too dangerous? Was it worth the costs?

The Supreme Court, however, had no doubts. In September 1958 it ruled that even with the threat of violence, desegregation of schools must go on.

In response, Governor Faubus next ordered all Arkansas public schools closed. Across the South, other school districts followed his example. For the moment, white resistance showed no signs of diminishing. Observes C. Vann Woodward:

> Desegregation of public schools in the South came virtually to a halt. In the first three years after the *Brown* decision, 712 school districts were desegregated, but in the last three years of the

Eisenhower Administration the number fell to 13 in 1958, 19 in 1959, and 17 in 1960.[53]

National Resistance

The South was not alone in its opposition to federally mandated integration. Much of the rest of the nation reacted with either indifference or criticism to the Supreme Court's decisions. Many northern lawyers and judges, for instance, severely disparaged the Supreme Court for its activism in promoting civil rights. Neither major political party championed civil rights issues. At the federal level, Eisenhower made it

President Eisenhower Speaks to the Nation

On September 25, 1957, President Dwight D. Eisenhower spoke to the nation about the racial disturbance in Little Rock, Arkansas. The president's concern for America's reputation abroad is seen in this following passage taken from his "Address on Little Rock" which appears in Documentary History of the Modern Civil Rights Movement, *edited by Peter B. Levy.*

"In the South, as elsewhere, citizens are keenly aware of the tremendous disservice that has been done to the people of Arkansas in the eyes of the nation, and that has been done to the nation in the eyes of the world.

At a time when we face grave situations abroad because of the hatred that communism bears toward a system of government based on human rights, it would be difficult to exaggerate the harm that is being done to the prestige and influence, and indeed to the safety, of our nation and the world.

Our enemies are gloating over this incident and using it everywhere to misrepresent our whole nation. We are portrayed as a violator of those standards of conduct which the people of the world united to proclaim in the Charter of the United Nations. There they affirmed 'faith in fundamental human rights' and 'in the dignity and worth of the human person' and they did so 'without distinction as to race, sex, language or religion.'

And so, with deep confidence, I call upon the citizens of the State of Arkansas to assist in bringing an immediate end to all interference with the law and its processes. If resistance to the federal court orders ceases at once, the further presence of federal troops will be unnecessary and the City of Little Rock will return to its normal habits of peace and order and a blot upon the fair name and high honor of our nation in the world will be removed.

Thus will be restored the image of America and all its parts as one nation, indivisible, with liberty and justice for all."

clear to the nation he did not favor an activist role for the federal government in the matter of civil rights.

Meanwhile, several members of Congress were actively hostile to the Supreme Court and tried unsuccessfully to enact laws that would nullify several of the Court's controversial civil rights decisions.

At this juncture, only the nation's courts kept an eye on racial injustice. These bodies would have much to say in the violent days yet to come.

Chapter

6 Confrontations

Late in the afternoon of February 1, 1960, four freshmen from the Agricultural and Technical College in Greensboro, North Carolina, sat down at the lunch counter in a nearby Woolworth department store and politely asked to be served coffee and doughnuts.

"We don't serve colored here,"[54] a waitress told them. Unfazed, the students remained seated and patiently waited until closing time. "Well, we'll have plenty of time tomorrow, because we'll be back,"[55] one of them told the store manager on the way out.

News of this staged "sit-in" spread quickly across the college campus. Recalls student and participant Franklin McCain:

As a matter of fact, word was back on campus before we ever got back. There were all sorts of phone calls to the administration and to people on the faculty and staff. The mayor's office was aware of it and the governor was aware of it. I think it was all over North Carolina within a matter of just an hour or so.[56]

The next day the four freshmen returned to the store with nineteen other

Four black college students sit at the Woolworth lunch counter insisting that they be served. The 1960 protest would serve as a model for blacks across the nation.

black students. Once again refused service, the students responded with another sit-in. Over and over this scene was replayed. Within a week, an estimated four hundred students were taking turns at the whites-only counter.

Word of the student action flashed across the South. Soon similar sit-ins were underway in towns and cities in thirteen states. By the fall of 1961, an estimated seventy thousand individuals were protesting segregation not only at lunch counters, but also in art galleries, courtrooms, libraries, theaters, beaches, and public swimming pools.

Most of the protestors were college-age blacks who had been children when the *Brown* case was decided. Having grown up expecting to enjoy full civil rights, they were angry that those rights were still denied them. And now, as young adults, many were ready to take bold action to make sure they did not wait much longer.

The Rise of Militants

Though advice and assistance poured in from CORE, the NAACP, and SCLC, many of the young crusaders flocked to a new organization, the Student Non-violent Coordinating Committee, or SNCC (pronounced snick), formed in April 1960. More militant than older civil rights organizations, SNCC was nonetheless committed to the same principles of Christian love and nonviolence advocated by Martin Luther King.

SNCC was also willing to challenge the authority of veteran civil rights leaders. Increasingly, America's black youths insisted on waging their own brand of protest, not that of their elders.

By 1960 the nation's political mood was shifting away from the rigid political conservatism of the previous decade. Prominent members of both major political parties publicly backed the sit-ins taking place around the country. And in 1961 a new president, Democrat John F. Kennedy, came to the Oval Office with a personal pledge to support the cause of black civil rights.

Meanwhile, however, legions of white segregationists remained unmoved. The more vicious among them still beat, kicked, and humiliated peaceful black demonstrators anywhere they tested the limits of Jim Crow. This fact was confirmed when several civil rights activists decided to challenge segregationists in the wake of another Supreme Court ruling.

Freedom Riders

In 1961 the Supreme Court banned segregation at the rest areas of the nation's railroad stations and bus terminals. The ruling extended a 1947 decision that outlawed segregation on trains and buses. Despite this ruling, however, most blacks in the Deep South continued to ride in segregated compartments and stand in segregated waiting rooms. Tradition and fear were too deeply rooted in this region to permit change. In addition, neither state nor federal officials ever enforced the court's antisegregation rulings.

On May 4, 1961, two commercial buses—a Greyhound and a Trailways—departed Washington, D.C. On board were young white and black CORE volunteers soon known as Freedom Riders. They were headed south—all the way to New Orleans—to test compliance with the

James Farmer and the First Freedom Ride

In this passage from Juan Williams's Eyes on the Prize, *CORE leader James Farmer recalls his hesitancy to take part in one of the first Freedom Rides.*

"I had decided that I was not going to take that ride from Montgomery to Jackson because I was scared. I didn't think the buses would arrive in Jackson safely. I had all kinds of excuses; my father had just died, and two deaths in the same week would have been a bit much for [my] family. Furthermore I had been away from my office for six weeks. None of the students— these were the SNCC students and the few CORE students from Nashville—ever asked me if I was going. They merely assumed I was going because, after all, it was my project. I had started it, and I had gone to Montgomery to join them. I went down to say goodbye to the students who were going to ride to Jackson. I reached my hand through an open window to shake hands with a young CORE girl from New Orleans, Doris Castle, who was seventeen years old at the time.

Her eyes were wide with fear. I said, 'Well, Doris, have a safe journey. After the Freedom Ride we'll get together in New Orleans or someplace and we'll have a big bowl of crab gumbo and we'll talk about the next step.' She looked at me with total disbelief and said, 'but Jim, you're going with us, aren't you?' I said, 'Well, no Doris,' and went through the whole catalog of reasons. Doris said just two words. In a stage whisper, she said, 'Jim. *Please.*' Well, that was more than I could bear. I said to a CORE aide, 'Get my luggage and put it on the bus. I'm going.'"

CORE leader James Farmer in 1964.

Court's ruling. Only minor encounters occurred when black Freedom Riders tried to use white facilities at rest stops in Virginia and North Carolina. But more serious trouble occurred at the bus terminal in Rock Hill, South Carolina, where a gang of angry white males attacked several riders. Adhering to their philosophy of nonviolence, the CORE volunteers stoically refused to hit back.

A Terrifying Incident

No further major incidents took place until May 14, the tenth day of the trip, when the Greyhound pulled into a bus station in Anniston, Alabama. Suddenly, a gang of hostile whites threw stones, banged on the bus with fists and iron bars, and slashed its tires. Carloads of whites followed the bus as it left. When a flat tire caused the bus to halt six miles outside the city limits, the attackers smashed bus windows and threw a firebomb into the vehicle. Passenger Genevieve Hughes recalls the terror of the incident:

> [A man] thrust a bundle, seemingly of rags through the window opposite me, at the same time lighting it. There was a noise, sparks flew and a dense cloud of smoke immediately filled the bus. I thought it was only a smoke bomb and climbed over the back of the seat. The smoke became denser and denser becoming completely black. I crouched and figured I was going to be asphyxiated.[57]

When the choking students fled the bus through an emergency exit, the white roughnecks beat and clubbed them. They halted their attack only when a white man,

Eli Cowling, fired a pistol into the air and threatened to kill anyone who delivered another blow. Cowling, an undercover Alabama state patrolman, had boarded the bus in Atlanta. Though he was no friend of the civil rights movement, he had no intention of watching murder.

In shock, the Freedom Riders watched their bus burn to a charred shell. Twelve of the group were treated at a local hospital for injuries and smoke inhalation. The students had no choice but to finish their journey to Birmingham in cars.

Meanwhile, violence awaited the second group of Freedom Riders on the Trailways bus as it pulled into the Anniston bus terminal. Here, they too were attacked by white hoodlums.

At the next stop in Birmingham, the students were besieged again, this time by a screaming mob wielding fists and metal pipes. Some Freedom Riders fell senseless to the ground. A white CORE member named Jim Peck required fifty stitches to close a head laceration.

In both Anniston and Birmingham, despite warnings of possible trouble, the local police were nowhere in sight when the fighting began.

Yet the Freedom Riders vowed to finish their journey. "I think it's particularly important at this time when it has become national news that we continue and show that non-violence can prevail over violence,"[58] Jim Peck told a reporter in Birmingham. Frightened bus drivers, however, were not willing to drive them any farther. At last, the students gave up and flew the rest of the way to New Orleans.

White racists had smashed the Freedom Ride, but they had not wiped out the spirit that motivated it. When news of the beatings flashed across the world, stu-

Freedom Riders view their bus after it was attacked and set afire by a white mob.

dents and older adults, both black and white, poured into Birmingham to embark on their own Freedom Rides. Some of the first to arrive were promptly arrested by Birmingham police, driven to the Alabama-Tennessee state line and abandoned on a country road late at night. Undeterred, they made their way back to Birmingham and boarded a bus for Montgomery.

Trouble waited there, too. When civil rights workers arrived on May 20, more than one thousand whites rioted in the streets of Montgomery and brutally beat students, local blacks and journalists, and sympathetic whites for nearly two hours.

During the attack, they also severely injured a federal official sent by President Kennedy to observe the situation and left him lying unconscious on the ground for twenty minutes. Again, local police were conspicuously absent.

TV coverage of the bloody melee shocked the nation, as racial tension mounted in Montgomery and the rest of Alabama. Chaos reigned during the next two days. The Alabama Associated Press denounced "the breakdown of civilized rule"[59] in Alabama.

Only after Kennedy sent six hundred federal marshals to Montgomery to protect the Freedom Riders and those who rallied in their support did Alabama governor John Patterson declare martial law in Alabama and secure public order. To avoid further bloodshed, federal officials tried to convince the Freedom Riders to call off the next leg of their journey into Mississippi, a state many civil rights workers considered more segregated and dangerous than Alabama. But the young activists would not be deterred.

Next, the president's brother, Attorney General Robert Kennedy, called upon Martin Luther King to use his influence to "cool off" the crusade. This request angered some black activists. "I asked Dr. King to tell Bobby Kennedy that we'd been cooling off for 350 years, and that if we cooled off anymore, we'd be in a deep freeze,"[60] remembers James Farmer of CORE.

Robert Kennedy tried once more to avoid violence. This time he conferred with officials in Mississippi and struck a controversial deal. Instead of enforcing the constitutional rights of the Freedom Riders to travel where they wanted, the attorney general agreed that Mississippi could enforce its segregation laws, if state officials ensured the safety of the riders.

As a result, no mobs were present when the buses arrived in Jackson, Mississippi, a few days later. A throng of police officers, however, was on hand to enforce Mississippi's segregation laws. This meant that any blacks who entered the white waiting room at the bus station were promptly arrested and jailed in sweltering Mississippi cells where many were beaten and tormented by guards. Within a few months, 328 Freedom Riders were jailed.

CORE's Freedom Riders had begun their journey to test compliance with new federal laws. They discovered that the white power structure in the Deep South ignored these laws and denied federal au-

A group of Freedom Riders waits to board a bus in Birmingham, Alabama, to continue its tour of the United States. President Kennedy sent six hundred federal marshals to protect the riders.

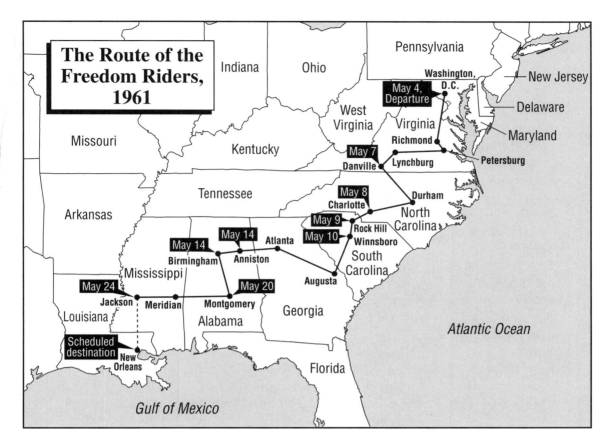

The Route of the Freedom Riders, 1961

Pennsylvania

Indiana

Ohio

Washington, D.C.

New Jersey

May 4, Departure

Delaware

West Virginia

Virginia

Maryland

Missouri

Richmond

Kentucky

May 7

Petersburg

Danville

Lynchburg

Tennessee

May 8

Charlotte

Durham

Arkansas

May 9

Rock Hill

North Carolina

May 14

May 14

Atlanta

May 10

Winnsboro

Birmingham

Anniston

South Carolina

Mississippi

Augusta

May 24

May 20

Jackson

Meridian

Montgomery

Georgia

Louisiana

Alabama

Atlantic Ocean

Scheduled destination

New Orleans

Florida

Gulf of Mexico

thority with impunity. But the Freedom Rides had not been in vain. The bravery of the students, clergymen, and others who ventured to Alabama in the summer of 1961 exposed many social wrongs and aroused the conscience of the nation.

The rides also succeeded in prompting the federal government to enforce the constitutional rights of African Americans. In September, the Interstate Commerce Commission issued regulations that forced bus companies across the nation to obey the Supreme Court's ban on segregated terminals and railroad stations. As a result, separate restrooms and waiting rooms in the South disappeared.

Help from the federal government would be needed again and again as

blacks dared to cross the color line—as one man discovered when he acted alone in Mississippi.

Standing Alone in Mississippi

In September 1962 federal courts ordered the University of Mississippi to admit its first black student, James Meredith, an Air Force veteran and a native of the state. University officials had successfully resisted past attempts at desegregation; so too had state lawmakers and judges. Meredith's most powerful foe was Mississippi governor Ross Barnett, a diehard segregationist who threatened to arrest any federal

Emotions Heat Up over Need to Cool Off

Many civil rights activists were incensed over Robert Kennedy's demand that Freedom Riders "cool off"—or call off—their provocative bus trips. Aldon D. Morris's The Origins of the Civil Rights Movement *contains Freedom Rider and CORE leader James Farmer's description of a heated exchange between activists and Attorney General Kennedy.*

"I was in jail in Mississippi. Bobby Kennedy called a meeting of CORE and SNCC, in his office. I could not be there, of course. I was in the clink. But several people from CORE went. And several people from SNCC went, just those two because these were the activist groups in the Freedom Rides. This was in the summer of '61. And at that meeting, what Bobby said to them according to the reports [was], 'Why don't you guys cut out all that . . . Freedom Riding and sitting-in [obscenity] and concentrate on voter education.' Says, 'If you do that I'll get you a tax exemption.' That cold-blooded. This was Bobby Kennedy. Says, '[W]ork on voter registration. If you do that I'll get you tax exemption.'

The SNCC guy almost hit him [Kennedy]. One of the SNCC guys and Bobby Kennedy were standing in the middle of the floor, in the middle of the office, they tell me, forehead to forehead, shouting at each other. It looked like they were going to start throwing punches some time. And one of the CORE people stepped in between them, had to pull them apart. SNCC was outraged, you know. 'Tell us that we concentrate on voter registration when we're fighting a tiger down there in Mississippi and Alabama. You're trying to buy us off.'"

official who interfered with Mississippi's segregation laws. Barnett himself personally blocked Meredith's attempt to register at the university's campus in Oxford.

Barnett's defiance provoked a strong federal response. On September 30, President Kennedy made a televised appeal to Mississippians not to disobey federal law. Meanwhile, 320 federal marshals escorted Meredith to his dormitory.

"It's difficult to believe that you are in the center of the most serious constitutional crisis ever experienced by the United States since the War of Secession [the Civil War],"[61] Paul Guihard, a French journalist, observed of the growing crisis.

These steps ignited a violent reaction from segregationists. That night a screaming mob of twenty-five hundred people swarmed across the university campus and battled federal marshals with bricks, clubs, gasoline bombs, and firearms. Many shocked observers realized that this riot was more than a protest against integration; it was an uprising against the federal government. Bloody fighting continued all night. By dawn two were dead, and nearly four hundred were injured. One of those killed was journalist Paul Guihard.

The violence at Oxford failed to stop the desegregation effort. Once again the federal government had demonstrated its willingness to enforce federal civil rights laws. Moreover, the rioting only underscored how far blacks had yet to go to achieve equality and acceptance.

White defiance still raged across the South. And nowhere was this more true than in Birmingham, Alabama, the South's most segregated city.

Mississippi state troopers stand by as a student yells insults at James Meredith.

Birmingham

For years, the white power structure in Birmingham ignored all efforts to banish Jim Crow. Schools, hospital wards, libraries, and bus terminals remained segregated. The city's belligerent police chief, Eugene "Bull" Connor, a well-known segregationist, ordered the closing of munici-

pal playgrounds, golf courses, and parks rather than desegregate them. Blacks could not dine alongside whites in restaurants, could not try on clothes in department stores before buying them, and were denied high-paying jobs in both business and government.

James Meredith is flanked by U.S. marshals as he enters the University of Mississippi in 1962. Such scenes, televised throughout the nation, led to a public awareness of blacks' courage and fortitude during the fight to end segregation.

A soldier injured by flying glass during the forced integration of the University of Mississippi is consoled by an officer. Hundreds of federal troops were sent to the university to quell rioting.

White supremacists held Birmingham in their grip. The local chapter of the Ku Klux Klan was powerful and popular. Since the end of World War II, terrorists had bombed fifty black homes and churches. Not one of these crimes had been solved, nor were they likely to be solved, given the brutality and openly expressed racist views of Bull Connor and many of the local police.

Birmingham's hard-core defiance, however, made it an ideal target for a major desegregation campaign.

Project C Unfolds

In the spring of 1963, several top civil rights leaders met at the Gaston Motel in Birmingham to plan Project C, a code name for "confrontation." Their goal was to tear Jim Crow down in Birmingham.

On April 3, Reverend Fred Shuttlesworth, founder of the Alabama Christ-

ian Movement for Human Rights, along with Dr. King and Reverend Ralph Abernathy of the SCLC, led hundreds of blacks into the streets on the first round of a large-scale nonviolent protest that included marches, boycotts, pickets, sit-ins, and a voter registration drive.

Bull Connor responded by ordering mass arrests of the demonstrators. But the next day hundreds of new marchers took their places in the streets demanding justice. Day after day the marches continued, growing steadily. Police arrested hundreds at a time. On April 13, King, Shuttlesworth, and Abernathy were jailed for ignoring a court order to stop the protests. While a prisoner in an overcrowded jail, King penned a lengthy response to a letter from a group of Alabama clergymen criticizing his action. "I am in Birmingham because injustice is here,"[62] he wrote.

On May 3, civil rights leaders approved a controversial move to permit thousands of black schoolchildren to march in Birmingham's streets. That evening the entire nation—and viewers around the world—sat before their television sets, shocked at images of black youngsters, along with black and white adults, assaulted by high-powered fire hoses, tear gas, attack dogs, and police clubs.

Infuriated by these attacks, many Birmingham blacks rejected pleas for nonviolence and pelted police with stones and bottles. Birmingham edged toward chaos.

As expressions of outrage and demands for action continued to pour into Washington, President Kennedy dispatched Assistant Attorney General Burke Marshall to Birmingham to find a way to stop the violence. Working around the clock, Marshall managed to negotiate with black leaders to come up with a shaky truce between the demonstrators and Birmingham's business community.

"The city of Birmingham has come to an accord with its conscience," [63] Shuttlesworth and King jointly announced. The negotiated agreement required civil rights leaders to halt the protest; in return, local business leaders, many of whom had been hurt economically by the boycotts, promised to desegregate their shops, lunch counters, and drinking fountains. They also vowed to hire more blacks in better-paying jobs.

Many Alabama whites scorned the accord. The Ku Klux Klan held a cross-burning ceremony and denounced King and the other civil rights leaders. Within

James Meredith Remembers

This reminiscence of civil rights pioneer James Meredith appears in Eyewitnesses and Others. *Meredith describes the turbulence that greeted his arrival at the University of Mississippi in October 1962.*

"When we were turned away the first time I tried to register at the university, and especially the second time, at the State Capitol in Jackson, I saw the mobs and heard them jeering, 'Go home, nigger' and that stuff, but I never recognized them as individuals at all, even those who showed the greatest contempt for me. I felt they were not personally attacking me but that they were protesting a change and this was something they felt they must do. I thought it was impersonal. Some of them were crying, and their crying indicated to me even more the pain of change and the fear of things they did not know. I feel the people were keyed up by the actions of their leaders. With Gov. Ross Barnett taking the position he did, the people were bound to act that way, and it didn't really have anything to do with me personally. That's the way I saw it."

an hour after the meeting with Marshall adjourned, dynamite explosions damaged the home of King's brother, A. D. King. Two more bombs blew up in the Gaston Motel.

News of the explosions sent blacks back into the streets of Birmingham. For three hours, they set fires and battled police. Not until three thousand federal troops arrived was order restored. But as Birmingham quieted, more violence brewed elsewhere in Alabama and the South.

Rising Violence

Trouble flared up on June 10 when a federal judge ordered the University of Alabama to open its doors to two black students. Alabama's new governor, George Wallace, an ardent segregationist, vowed to personally block their entrance into the university. President Kennedy responded by informing Wallace that he was prepared to use federal force to enforce the court order. Nonetheless, Wallace staged a confrontation as he had promised. He quickly yielded to the students, however, when Kennedy put the Alabama National Guard under federal authority.

Kennedy took further action. The next night, he delivered an address to the American people that focused on the rising racial violence and the need to protect black civil rights:

> The events in Birmingham and elsewhere have so increased the cries for equality that no city or state or legislative body can . . . ignore them. . . . We face . . . a moral crisis as a country and a people. It cannot be met by re-

pressive police action. It cannot be left to increased demonstrations in the streets. . . . It is a time to act in the Congress, in your state and local legislative body, and above all, in all our daily lives.[64]

The very next day Medgar Evers, field secretary of the NAACP in Mississippi, was gunned down outside his home while his wife and two children trembled in horror inside. When his accused murderer was freed after two mistrials, racial disorder erupted in Maryland, Florida, Virginia, North Carolina, and Pennsylvania.

The uprisings were part of a wave of turmoil between the races that swept the South in the summer of 1963. As many as 758 black protests and uprisings occurred in numerous towns and cities following the truce in Birmingham.

Civil rights leader Medgar Evers was slain in front of his family in Mississippi. The mistrials of his accused murderer led to violent protests throughout the South.

At this point, two civil rights veterans, A. Philip Randolph and Bayard Rustin, realized something more than confrontation was needed to keep the movement going. They sent out a nationwide call for participation in something big that would mark the civil rights movement's finest hour—a massive demonstration in Washington, D.C.

The Big March

Assisting Randolph and Rustin in planning this huge event were the leaders of the NAACP, SCLC, CORE, and the National Urban League, along with officials of several labor organizations. These leaders wanted to create a forum in the nation's capital where speakers could vent grievances, set goals, and boost the flagging spirits of civil rights workers. Specifically, they wanted the march to show support for the comprehensive Civil Rights Act that Kennedy had recently sent to Congress. In addition, writes Juan Williams, the goals of the march included demands for "integration of public schools by year's end; enactment of a fair employment practices bill prohibiting job discrimination; and [a] demand for job training and placement."[65]

On August 28, 1963, a quarter of a million Americans gathered before the Lincoln Memorial. Though most were African Americans, they were joined by people of many races, creeds, ages, and backgrounds. They had arrived by every means of transportation possible, including 1,514 chartered buses and 21 special trains.

Many carried signs with messages such as "We Demand an End to Bias Now" and "We March for Integrated Schools Now." A multitude of voices sang out the words of

A quarter of a million Americans march on Washington to support black civil rights on August 28, 1963.

what was now the anthem of the civil rights movement:

> We shall overcome
> We shall overcome
> We shall overcome someday.
> Oh, deep in my heart
> We shall overcome someday.

On that warm, cloudless summer day, marchers heard a variety of singers and speakers. But the most memorable performance came from Martin Luther King, who delivered a moving speech that would

I Have a Dream

King's "I Have a Dream" speech, delivered at the March on Washington, August 28, 1963, has thrilled listeners and readers for decades. This sampling is taken from a transcript found in Leon Friedman's The Civil Rights Reader.

"I have a dream that my four little children will one day live in a nation where they will not be judged by the color of their skin but by the content of their character.

I have a dream today.

I have a dream that one day the state of Alabama . . . will be transformed into a situation where little black boys and black girls will be able to join hands with little white boys and white girls and walk together as sisters and brothers.

I have a dream today.

I have a dream that one day every valley shall be exalted, every hill and mountain shall be made low, the rough places will be made plains, and the crooked places will be made straight, and the glory of the Lord shall be revealed, and all flesh shall see it together."

Martin Luther King Jr. delivers his address at the Lincoln Memorial civil rights march, which he called "the greatest demonstration of freedom in the history of our nation."

stir the minds of people around the world. It also reminded everyone of the overriding purpose of the civil rights movement. He proclaimed: "I have a dream that one day this nation will rise up and live out the true meaning of its creed: 'We hold these truths to be self-evident; that all men are created equal.'"[66]

King's rousing speech ended the day on a note of optimism. But just five days later

Martin Luther King Jr. and others march for black civil rights in Washington, D.C.

euphoria gave way to anger and fear when trouble once again erupted in Birmingham.

Tragedy in Birmingham

On September 2, Alabama's Governor Wallace once again defied federal authorities by ordering state troopers and National Guardsmen to seal off Birmingham's schools to prevent them from becoming integrated. Again Kennedy intervened to keep the schools open.

Suddenly, on the morning of September 15, a bomb exploded at Birmingham's Sixteenth Street Baptist Church. In the basement, amid the rubble of broken bricks and stained glass, lay the bodies of four black girls whose ages ranged from eleven to fourteen. The young girls had been attending Sunday school when the explosion killed them.

The incident sparked a violent reaction in Birmingham with enraged blacks attacking whites and setting fire to white businesses. But other blacks beseeched the city to remain calm. Chris McNair, father of the youngest victim, told his angry neighbors, "We must not let this change us into something different than who we are. We must be human."[67]

Meanwhile, white supremacist leader Connie Lynch taunted, "They're just little niggers . . . and if there's four less niggers tonight, then I say, 'Good for whoever planted the bomb!'"[68]

Before the day was over two more black youths lay dead. Police shot a sixteen-year-old boy in a rock-throwing incident, and another thirteen-year-old boy was murdered by two white teenagers who had attended a segregationist rally earlier that day.

A President Is Slain

Little more than two months after the tragedies in Birmingham, President Kennedy was also dead, a victim of assassination. With his passing, the civil rights movement lost a powerful ally. Coretta King, wife of Dr. King, recalls:

> We felt that President Kennedy had been a friend of the cause and that with him as President we could continue to move forward. We watched and prayed for him. Then it was announced that the President was dead. Martin had been very quiet during this period. Finally he said, "This is what is going to happen to me also. . . ."[69]

Activists' personal grief was deepened by the knowledge that Kennedy had not yet prevailed in pushing through his new civil rights legislation, the most comprehensive bill in a hundred years. A new president was now in power—Lyndon Baines Johnson, a southerner.

Johnson Backs the Civil Rights Bill

Unlike most other southern politicians of this era, however, Johnson was fully committed to implementing civil rights. Known as a shrewd politician, he used his legendary skills of persuasion and deal making to fight for passage of a major civil rights bill.

Johnson did not fight alone. He was joined in an intense lobbying effort by a vast array of liberal groups and civil rights organizations. Religious institutions such as the Catholic Interracial Council, the National Council of Churches, the Jewish Anti-Defamation League of B'nai-B'rith, and the Quakers also lobbied in favor of the bill.

Meanwhile, white segregationists and their various organizations struggled des-

President Lyndon Johnson signs the Civil Rights Act of 1964, abolishing Jim Crow laws.

perately to kill the bill. During several months of hard and angry debate, over 560 amendments were proposed to change the language of the bill, usually to weaken it. Most of these attempts failed.

Finally, on July 2 President Johnson signed the Civil Rights Act of 1964 into law. With a stroke of the pen, the federal government had delivered a fatal blow to the legality of Jim Crow. Racial discrimination in places of public accommodations such as motels, restaurants, and theaters was now banned.

But how would the South react? Would the southern white power structure become even more defiant? More violent? The nation waited anxiously for its response.

7 Battle for the Ballot

The South did not react violently to the new civil rights law, as many had feared. Despite small disturbances, many theaters, restaurants, and other places of public accommodation opened their doors to blacks without major incident.

But all too soon, many civil rights workers realized that the sweeping new legislation had failed to appropriately address the vital issue of voting. A great majority of southern blacks still did not vote. The use of poll taxes, literacy tests, economic reprisal, and terror still cowed millions of blacks. Aaron Henry, an NAACP leader in Mississippi, explained the common plight of most blacks in his home state:

Any step which will bring a Negro into the public view, will increase the likelihood that an employer, or a creditor, or a landlord will deprive him of the economic necessities.

This problem is [made worse] by the extreme degree of poverty which exists among the Negro communities of Mississippi. To take an economic risk in Mississippi is to risk life itself.[70]

Amid abject poverty, most adult blacks were also disenfranchised. Though they made up nearly half of the state's population, they comprised only 5 percent of all registered voters. As long as blacks were

A black woman proudly casts her vote in the presidential election in 1964. The Civil Rights Act of 1964 did not end all of the discrimination blacks encountered in the South.

denied the vote, the wretched conditions in which they lived were unlikely to change.

But by 1964, the winds of change were blowing—from outside the state. A consensus developed within the civil rights community that Mississippi was to be the next battleground. Here, the fight would be to register blacks to vote.

The Mississippi Summer Freedom Project

SNCC had already penetrated Mississippi with a voter registration drive in 1960 led by former New York teacher Robert Moses. One of Moses's first steps was to set up a campaign to educate Mississippi's blacks to prepare them to pass Mississippi's literacy tests.

In the summer of 1964, this voting drive expanded when the SCLC teamed up with SNCC and formed a new organization called the Council of Federated Organizations (COFO). When word went out that the COFO needed help for its ambitious Mississippi Summer Freedom Project, more than one thousand young people from across the nation volunteered to help. The majority of these volunteers were idealistic northern white college students willing to spend their summers tutoring blacks and heading up discussion groups on a host of topics.

Mississippi's white power structure reacted negatively to the arrival of these eager volunteers from the North. Writes Benjamin Muse in *The American Negro Revolution*:

Mississippi prepared angrily for the "invasion." The state legislature passed a spate of new laws to . . . keep Negroes and white crusaders under control. The State Highway Patrol was increased from 275 to 475 men, municipalities were given new authority to restrain movements of individuals and to pool police forces and equipment, penalties for violating city ordinances were increased, and heavy fines were prescribed for refusal to comply with police commands in . . . circumstances relating specifically to the tactics of civil-rights demonstrators.[71]

Mississippi's White Knights, the most violent white supremacist group in the region, also prepared for battle against the college students. Imperial Wizard Sam Bowers urged his men to wage "counter attacks" against "selected individuals."[72]

To prepare the inexperienced civil rights workers for the trouble that awaited them, the National Council of Churches sponsored training sessions in Oxford, Ohio, where SNCC officials taught nonviolent tactics and self-defense techniques for the dangers that lay ahead.

Such precautions proved necessary. Before the summer ended, white terrorists had bombed thirty homes, torched thirty-seven black churches, and beaten at least eighty civil rights workers. In addition, Mississippi law enforcement officers arrested over one thousand activists, usually on trumped-up charges. The story that rocked the nation that summer, however, focused on three young male volunteers—two whites and one black—who disappeared in Neshoba County, Mississippi.

Neshoba County sheriff Lawrence Rainey attempted to downplay the disappearance of the men: "If they're missing, they just hid somewhere, trying to get a lot of publicity."[73] But six weeks later, after a

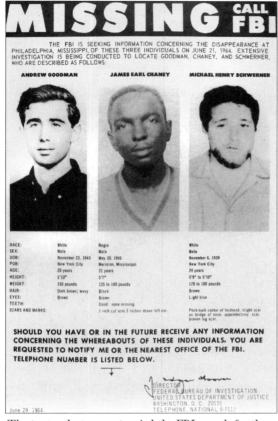

The poster that accompanied the FBI search for three civil rights workers. The murdered corpses of all three were found buried in Mississippi.

massive manhunt, FBI agents found the corpses of Michael Schwerner, Andrew Goodman, and James Chaney buried deep under several feet of Mississippi red clay. Authorities determined that the young men had been kidnapped and murdered. Condemnation and expressions of concern immediately filled the national airwaves. Often, though, the discussion was divided along racial lines. Many blacks bitterly observed that it took the deaths of two young white adults to provoke national outrage. Where was the national conscience over the deaths of hundreds of blacks over the decades? they wondered.

This argument was often expressed after the manhunt for the civil rights workers also turned up the mangled bodies of two young black Mississippians, Charles Moore and Henry Dee, who had been missing since early May. Their disappearances were scarcely noticed by the general public.

Some civil rights leaders, however, had actually anticipated that violent deaths of white volunteers would help the movement. They had correctly predicted that attacks on the children of America's white middle class would focus national attention on the injustices blacks faced every day.

Eventually twenty-one men, including Sheriff Rainey, were arrested in connection with the murders. But eventually, charges of murder were dropped against all the suspects. Civil rights workers, however, did manage to bring federal charges of civil rights violations against twelve of the men. During their trial, several of the accused exhibited smugness and leering defiance. Like many other white Mississippians, they seemed convinced that no white jury would ever convict them.

They were wrong. The jury convicted seven of the men, who later received prison sentences ranging from three to ten years.

No justice was forthcoming in connection with the murders of Moore and Dee, however. Although a white racist confessed to killing the men, a Mississippi judge dropped all charges.

Summer's End

At the end of the summer of 1964, most of the volunteers returned to their home states. They left behind 150 students and 200 SNCC and CORE workers to carry on the work.

Though the Summer Freedom Project had not radically altered life for Mississippi blacks, it had made progress. Explains Benjamin Muse, "The morale of Mississippi Negroes had received a tremendous lift. Many had been made to feel the dignity and joy of manly protest; new leaders had come forward. A political consciousness had been awakened."[74]

And this new political consciousness was growing stronger every day. By August an estimated eighty thousand Mississippi blacks were taking part in various civil rights campaigns in their state. Because Mississippi's Democratic Party was off limits to blacks, many African Americans joined a new political party, the Mississippi Freedom Democrats (MFD), which opened its membership to people of all races.

Despite the hard work of the Freedom Democrats, black voter registration remained low in Mississippi. It was not much better elsewhere in the Deep South. In Alabama, for instance, the number of voters increased from 6,000 in 1947 to 110,000 in 1964. But 70 percent of eligible black voters remained unregistered. In some Alabama counties, no blacks were registered. The situation was scarcely better in the Alabama city of Selma, the site of the next major civil rights confrontation.

Selma

Selma blacks made up half of the city's population, but comprised only 1 percent of the voters. Civil rights workers in Selma and nearby Marion had been attempting to improve these numbers since 1963. But their efforts had largely failed. Powerful white interests, using the same methods found elsewhere in the South, kept African Americans intimidated. Local police physically intercepted blacks trying to enter the

Hundreds of young blacks continue to sing freedom songs following their mass arrest for peacefully protesting in front of the Dallas County courthouse in Selma, Alabama.

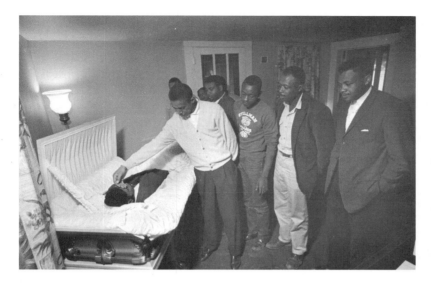

Mourners view the body of Jimmie Lee Jackson, who died after a state trooper shot him during a protest march. Jackson's death caused some civil rights leaders to rethink the passive resistance model advocated by Martin Luther King Jr.

courthouse to register to vote. Anyone who managed to enter the building generally discovered that the registrar's office was closed—at least when blacks were present.

Selma's reputation made it the target of a major voting campaign. In January 1965, SNCC and the SCLC pooled their resources and descended on the city for a showdown on voting rights. Among the luminaries of the movement who arrived was Martin Luther King, who had recently received the Nobel Peace Prize.

Day after day, marchers sang, prayed, and marched through the streets of Selma and implored local blacks to register. But Sheriff Jim Clark, a racist lawman whose behavior and demeanor rivaled that of Alabama's Bull Connor, ordered his officers to stop any demonstrator who got too near the courthouse. Over a period of weeks, his men arrested nearly two thousand marchers, including King and other civil rights leaders.

These arrests did not stop the campaign. Instead, the protest spread to communities beyond Selma. On February 18, the crusade suffered its first casualty at Marion, twenty-five miles from Selma, when a state trooper shot and killed Jimmie Lee Jackson, a black laborer, who attacked a policeman who had clubbed Jackson's mother during a protest march.

Civil rights leaders had to work hard to keep Jackson's death from turning the demonstrators to violence. At the funeral service Dr. King observed, "Jimmie Lee Jackson's death . . . must prove that unmerited does not go unredeemed. We must not be bitter and we must not harbor ideas of retaliating with violence. We must not lose faith in our white brothers." [75]

But Jackson's death also compelled civil rights leaders to rethink their efforts. So far the campaign in Selma seemed to be going nowhere. It was time, they decided, to adopt a new, bold strategy.

The March

It was Martin Luther King who made the impassioned appeal to the nation for help. He asked America to send volunteers to escort him and his fellow civil rights activists on a fifty-four-mile march to Alabama's state capital, Montgomery. Here, civil rights leaders intended to present their grievances to Alabama's political leaders and demand legal reform to prevent the abuses inflicted upon blacks by segregationists in Selma and elsewhere.

An alarmed Governor George Wallace declared in a news conference, "Such a march cannot and will not be tolerated."[76] Plans for the march continued nonetheless. On March 7, 1965, a group of five hundred marchers of all ages, races, and ethnic backgrounds, carrying bedrolls and satchels, set off alongside U.S. Route 80 for Montgomery.

Trouble soon appeared. Marchers had only progressed three hundred yards when they encountered opposition. Ahead of them waited Sheriff Clark's men and state troopers under the command of Alabama's director of public safety, Al Lingo. Some men were mounted on horseback. Others wore gas masks. Acting on instructions from the governor, Clark ordered the marchers to turn back to Selma. When they refused, the deputies discharged tear gas canisters. Then those on horseback charged the demonstrators and swung their nightsticks until they dispersed.

True to his word, Wallace had stopped the march. "But across the nation the incident set off an uproar the like of which had not been seen before in the history of the civil-rights movement,"[77] writes Benjamin Muse. Thunderous denunciations of Wallace and Alabama came from a multitude of religious, labor, government, and business leaders across America.

Civil rights leaders next went to court seeking to legally keep Wallace and law enforcement authorities from obstructing the march. Judge Frank M. Johnson ordered a temporary halt to the march until he gathered more information for a final decision.

But the marchers refused to wait. On March 9, they made another attempt. Once again they were confronted by police; this time, King called back his people before violence erupted. That night, however, three white clergymen from out of state who had arrived to take part in the march were attacked by whites in Selma. One of the men, Reverend James J. Reebs, a Unitarian minister from Boston, was beaten to death.

News of Reebs's death provoked further outrage outside the South. Within days tens of thousands of Americans representing a spectrum of races, ages, classes, and occupations poured into Alabama to take part in the march. "It is a terrible thing to say, but it took the death of a white clergyman to turn things around,"[78] observed Orloff Miller, another of the ministers attacked along with Reeb.

Meanwhile, in the nation's capital, President Johnson warily tracked these events. On March 15, he spoke to the nation in a televised address to Congress. One of his purposes for the speech was to ready the nation for a new voting rights bill he would submit in two days. But the president also voiced strong support for the Selma-to-Montgomery march:

> Even if we pass this bill, the battle will not be over. What happened in Selma is a part of a far larger movement which reaches into every section and state of America. It is the effort of American Negroes to secure for themselves the full blessings of American life.

Their cause must be our cause too. It is not just Negroes, but all of us, who must overcome the crippling legacy of bigotry and injustice. And we shall overcome.[79]

With the words "We shall overcome" Johnson effectively wedded the federal government to the civil rights movement.

On March 17, four days before the march was to resume, Judge Johnson issued his final decision on the marchers' lawsuit: The "proposed plan of march from Selma to Montgomery, Alabama, for its intended purposes, is clearly a reasonable exercise of a right guaranteed by the Constitution of the United States."[80]

The path was now legally clear for the march to begin. But Governor Wallace presented one last obstacle. On March 19, the governor informed the president that Alabama could not afford to pay for the six thousand National Guardsmen required to safeguard the marchers.

Johnson's response was swift and unambiguous. He ordered 1,800 Alabama National Guardsmen, 2,000 army troops, 100 FBI personnel, and 100 other federal

Fifteen Dr. Kings

In his book An Easy Burden, *civil rights activist and politician Andrew Young recalls a tense moment during the march to Montgomery in late March 1965.*

"The next day, Saturday, as we prepared to regroup for our march to the state capitol, John Doar of the Justice Department ran up to me and whispered, 'Andy, we have reports there's a sniper on the outskirts of Montgomery waiting to shoot Dr. King.'. . . Doar wanted us to remove Martin from the march and drive him into Montgomery to rejoin the march at the capitol.

Trying to get Martin to step out of the march for his own protection was impossible. . . .

But I felt there was something I could do. Most crazy white folks think all black folks look alike anyway, so I asked every preacher who had on a blue suit like Martin's to 'walk with Dr. King in the front row as we triumphantly enter the capital of Southern racism and bigotry.' About fifteen ministers rushed to situate themselves in the front row, all flanking Martin, all dressed alike. They never did find out why they were there. But they loved it. I'll never know for certain whether my plan foiled a would-be assassin that day. But in any case, Martin led the march as planned, and we walked into Montgomery without incident."

agents to escort the nearly 3,000 marchers who began the historic walk on March 21. Three days later, another 10,000 joined the march on the outskirts of Montgomery. And as the civil rights crusaders entered the city, their ranks swelled to 25,000.

Governor Wallace denounced the marchers when they arrived in Montgomery. He also refused to meet with any of their leaders. But his stubbornness had little effect on the tide of public opinion rolling against him. By now the eyes of the world had witnessed the huge, peaceful march for justice.

And the man who had led them, Martin Luther King, now said, "They told us we wouldn't get here. And there were those who said that we would get here only over their dead bodies. But all the world today knows that we are here, and that we are standing before the forces of power in the state of Alabama, saying 'we ain' let nobody turn us around.'"[81]

Despite predictions to the contrary, the march had also taken place without loss of life. But this good fortune ended abruptly the next day. Viola Gregg Liuzzo, a white thirty-nine-year-old Michigan mother of five, had come to Selma to help transport volunteers in her car. That evening three Klansmen spotted her on a remote country road with a black male civil rights worker

Martin Luther King Jr. leads the Selma-to-Montgomery civil rights march. With King are his wife, Coretta, and (on King's right) Dr. Ralph Bunche and Rev. Ralph Abernathy.

President Johnson Speaks to the Nation

A week after the attack on the marchers in Selma, Alabama, President Lyndon Johnson went on nationwide television to explain the provisions of the voting rights bill he was submitting to Congress. This sampling of the president's remarks is excerpted from Contemporary American Voices, *edited by James R. Andrews and David Zarefsky.*

"Every American citizen must have an equal right to vote. . . .

Yet the harsh fact is that in many places in this country men and women are kept from voting simply because they are Negroes. . . .

Every device of which human ingenuity is capable has been used to deny this right. . . .

Wednesday I will send to Congress a law designed to eliminate illegal barriers to the right to vote. . . .

This bill will strike down restriction to voting in all elections—Federal, State, and local—which have been used to deny Negroes the right to vote.

This bill will establish a simple, uniform standard which cannot be used, however ingenious the effort, to flout our Constitution. . . . [It] will ensure that properly registered individuals are not prohibited from voting. . . .

To those who seek to avoid action by their National Government in their own communities; who want to and who seek to maintain purely local control over elections, the answer is simple:

Open your polling places to all your people.

Allow men and women to register and vote whatever the color of their skin.

Extend the rights of citizenship to every citizen of this land."

passenger. They pulled up to her Oldsmobile and shot her to death.

Angered by Liuzzo's death, President Johnson denounced those who resorted to violence. But Johnson did even more. He fought hard for yet another civil rights law. Five months later, on August 6, Congress passed a historic piece of legislation, the Voting Rights Act of 1965, which Johnson signed into law on August 10. The new statute outlawed literacy tests and gave federal examiners the authority to register black voters in Alabama, Georgia, Louisiana, Mississippi, South Carolina, and Virginia.

That same year, the nation ratified the Twenty-fourth Amendment to the Constitution, barring the use of poll taxes in

James Meredith lies wounded after being shot by a sniper during his one-man "Walk Against Fear" from Memphis, Tennessee, to Jackson, Mississippi.

federal elections. The Supreme Court later banned them from state elections as well.

Historian Howard Zinn writes, "The effect on Negro voting in the South was dramatic. In 1952, a million southern blacks (20 percent of those eligible) registered to vote. In 1964 the number was 2 million—40 percent. By 1968, it was 3 million, 60 percent—the same percentage as white voters."[82]

Despite these legal gains, many African Americans remained too frightened to exercise their rights. Memories of the one hundred individuals killed since the *Brown* decision paralyzed them with fear.

Walk Against Fear

In 1966, James Meredith, the first black to graduate from the University of Mississippi, decided to meet this fear head on. In June he set out on a publicized one-

man walk from Memphis, Tennessee, to Jackson, Mississippi—a stretch overrun with white racists. Meredith wanted to publicly demonstrate his right to freedom of movement. In addition, he hoped to use his "Walk Against Fear" to encourage fellow blacks to register to vote.

But Meredith's journey ended abruptly the next day, when he was ambushed by a white man with a shotgun. Once again the American public exploded with anger. President Johnson ordered federal agents to track down the assailant and civil rights leaders flocked to the Memphis hospital where Meredith lay wounded. Black and white sympathizers banded together and took to the highway to finish the march on Meredith's behalf.

Varying in number from one hundred to fifteen hundred participants, the marchers spent the next three weeks in small towns and villages urging local blacks to register to vote. Though state troopers guarded them at times, the marchers often encountered violence and jeering. For instance, when Martin Luther King led a prayer service for the three civil rights workers murdered in Neshoba County, a white mob descended upon him and his followers with ax handles and hoes.

The tone of this march revealed something disturbing to civil rights leaders. Bickering was common. Black and white volunteers often argued with each other. By now, in fact, many blacks had become suspicious and resentful of white liberals who took part in the demonstrations. Heckling increased between the marchers and journalists who covered the event. Blacks also argued among themselves over the purpose and direction of the march. Through it all, observed journalist Renata Adler, King "proved on the march that he is still the leader of the movement, and perhaps the most forceful voice of conscience in the country. People came from all over Mississippi to see him, and responded to the measured, rational cadences of his voice."[83]

Nonetheless, many young blacks were also listening to a new voice. It belonged to a tall, lean young man of Trinidad descent from New York named Stokely Carmichael. A veteran Freedom Rider and voter registration organizer in Mississippi, Carmichael was smart, fiery, and militant. He had formed his own views on what direction the march—and the entire civil rights movement—should take. Carmichael and other young African Americans had begun to turn away from King's policy of nonviolence. Instead, they argued, it was time to fight back. They also had a new rallying cry: "Black Power!"

8 The Movement Splinters

The gulf between Martin Luther King and Stokely Carmichael mirrored the fundamental rift within the civil rights community that emerged when the "big five" civil rights groups failed to agree on the purpose of the Meredith march. The NAACP continued to strive for peaceful integration with whites. But SNCC's younger and increasingly militant rank-and-file favored separatism.

Until now, the civil rights movement had been mostly a southern phenomena. But by the mid-1960s, national attention began to shift to the North, where 37 percent of all blacks now lived. Armed with new civil rights laws, the federal government no longer confined its criticism to the South. Now it began to also address segregation problems in northern cities. Among its chief targets were the region's public schools. Ironically, as southern school districts desegregated, many in the North became more segregated.

Unlike the South, the North did not segregate by law. Income differences between blacks and whites partly explained this de facto segregation, but racism was also to blame. Many northern whites, for instance, refused to rent homes and apartments to blacks. Realtors commonly showed black clients only dwellings in black neighborhoods.

Panic struck many northern whites, including many who had supported desegregation efforts in the South, when desegregation efforts came to their own schools and neighborhoods. Many urban whites quickly sold their homes and moved to suburban neighborhoods where blacks were rare.

Like the South, the North also had white extremists who resorted to violence. King learned this brutal fact firsthand when he led his first northern crusade, a series of protest marches through all-white neighborhoods of Chicago demanding an open housing policy for the city in late July 1966.

In response, thousands of angry whites lined the streets and heckled and abused the marchers as they passed. Groups of thugs, incited by street-corner speakers from the Ku Klux Klan and the American Nazi Party, brandished signs saying "White Power" and pelted demonstrators with stones and bottles. Many of these toughs were of working-class, Eastern European extraction who had struggled to escape ghetto areas themselves. Now they feared an influx of poor blacks would turn their neighborhoods back into the very slums they had fled.

At times as many as twelve hundred local police were needed to keep the Chicago crowds under control. Surprised by the ugly reaction, King recalled, "I have seen many demonstrations in the South but I have never seen any so hostile and so hateful as I have seen here today. I have to do this—to expose myself—to bring this hate into the open."[84]

Rejecting Passive Resistance

Excerpted from his 1966 essay that appears in Eyewitnesses and Others, *Black Power advocate Stokely Carmichael makes this distinction between the Student Non-violent Coordinating Committee (SNCC) and Martin Luther King's movement.*

"One of the tragedies of the struggle against racism is that up to now there has been no national organization which could speak to the growing militancy of young black people in the urban ghetto.

There has been only a civil rights movement, whose tone of voice was adapted to an audience of liberal whites. It served as a sort of buffer zone between them and angry young blacks. None of its so-called leaders could go into a rioting community and be listened to. In a sense, I blame ourselves—together with the mass media—for what has happened in Watts, Harlem, Chicago, Cleveland, Omaha. Each time the people in those cities saw Martin Luther King get slapped, they became angry, when they saw four little black girls bombed to death, they were angrier, and when nothing happened, they were steaming. We had nothing to offer that they could see, except to go out and be beaten again. We helped to build their frustration.

For too many years, black Americans marched and had their heads broken and got shot. . . . We cannot be expected any longer to . . . say to whites: come on, you're nice guys. For you are not nice guys.

An organization which claims to speak for the needs of a community—as does the Student Non-violent Coordinating Committee—must speak in the tone of that community, not as somebody else's buffer zone. This is the significance of black power as a slogan. For once, black people are going to use the words they want to use—not just the words whites want to hear. And they will do this no matter how often the press tries to stop the use of the slogan by equating it with racism and separatism."

King's campaign—the Chicago Freedom Movement—achieved some success when city officials and county governments, along with other community leaders, agreed to implement a ten-step plan to improve open housing for local blacks.

But the march was disappointing. It revealed that northern blacks were less receptive to King's message of nonviolent protest than their southern counterparts. Civil rights pioneer Bayard Rustin, in fact, publicly wondered if King's methods could be effective outside the South. A civil rights movement steeped in religious sentiment made sense in the South. African Americans had always been able to rely on strong church-based communities for spiritual, emotional, and physical support during times of stress. And although inequality existed among the races in the South, there was also a strong familiarity. In the countless small towns and rural areas of Dixie, blacks and whites had known each other all their lives. And like rural people

everywhere, both races shared a strong sense of identity with the land and region where they lived.

But the black experience in the urban North was wholly different. In the big cities of New York, Chicago, Newark, and Detroit, the great majority of African Americans lived in rat-infested, dilapidated ghettos. Here most blacks lived largely isolated from whites. Uprooted and estranged from their southern origins, many had left behind strong family and community ties. Religion seldom was as powerful a force in their lives as it was for southern blacks. Intellectuals, rather than preachers, tended to be leaders in African American communities in the North.

Economic stress also kept northern blacks in a steady state of despair. In 1964 automation, the process of replacing unskilled and semi-skilled human workers with mechanized systems, cost the nation forty thousand jobs a week. Since a disproportionate share of these jobs were filled

In Chicago, Illinois, white hecklers taunt civil rights marchers who are protesting segregation in housing. Such attacks caused many civil rights leaders to advocate violence.

A dilapidated neighborhood sits just ten blocks from the Capitol. Because of racist housing policies, even affluent blacks could not escape the poorest neighborhoods.

by African Americans, black unemployment rates were double those of whites in the nation's big industrial cities.

Everywhere in the sprawling northern ghettos, blacks blamed their unhappy conditions on white racism and discrimination. Historian William Pitt points out that:

> Unlike the white immigrants who had made it out to the suburbs, blacks found that for all but a few of them, the ghetto was the end of the line. The majority were too poor to move on, and wherever they turned for better schools, neighborhoods, and jobs, they seemed to encounter the color bar.[85]

Ironically, the accomplishments of the civil rights movement in the South also contributed to a deep frustration among many blacks. The movement's triumphs in the courts and legislatures and on the streets raised expectations among many blacks that social and economic conditions would soon bring improvements to their communities. But these hopes quickly faded when life did not measurably improve. Many northern blacks concluded that the civil rights movement in the South was irrelevant to their lives. Access to public accommodations? Voting rights? Urban blacks often replied that these rights had been available in the North for years, but had done little to improve conditions for ghetto dwellers.

Finally, television also contributed to a general feeling of resentment among urban blacks. According to a 1968 government report on conditions in the American inner city: "Most whites and some Negroes outside the ghetto have prospered to a degree unparalleled in the history of civilization. Through television and other media, this affluence has been flaunted before the eyes of the Negro poor and the jobless ghetto youth."[86]

These contrasts, coupled with TV's relentless images of leering white racists and brutal beatings and teargassing of black men, women, and children in Mississippi, Alabama, and elsewhere in the South, kept blacks everywhere in a state of constant anger. As a result, many African Americans felt they had no other option but to use violence themselves to make their grievances heard.

Summers of Rage

The powder keg of black discontent finally exploded. In 1964 the first major disturbances took place in black sections of Philadelphia, Chicago, and New York City. A year later, on August 11, 1965, only five days after the passage of the Voting Rights Act, a mostly black area of Los Angeles called Watts erupted with four days of riots, death, and destruction.

The Watts riot was sparked by a single incident. About 7:00 P.M. that evening Marquette Frye, a black motorist, was pulled over by a highway patrolman on suspicion of reckless driving and arrested when he failed a sobriety test. Frye violently resisted the arrest. His brother and mother also fought the officers, as a group of blacks gathered nearby. Within a half hour, the group had become a crowd of over one thousand. By this time, more officers had arrived and arrested all three members of the Frye family, plus a young woman and a man, charged with inciting the mob to violence.

Exaggerated stories of police brutality quickly spread through the black community and ignited racial tensions. Soon, gangs of angry blacks began attacking white motorists.

Despite the efforts of community leaders to keep the peace, even worse violence erupted the next two evenings when thousands of young blacks rampaged through their own community, yelling "Burn, baby, burn" and smashing and setting fire to automobiles, houses, and businesses, many of them owned by other blacks. Here and there gunfire was exchanged between looters and police. Rioting, looting, and burning continued for three more days. When order was finally restored by nearly fourteen thousand California National Guardsmen, thirty-four people lay dead and more than one thousand were injured. Property losses were estimated at $40 million.

But Watts was only the beginning of a prolonged rash of major racial disturbances throughout the United States. From 1965 to 1968, an estimated 150 major riots along with many smaller violent incidents occurred in major American cities. Most of them were outside of the South, in cities such as Baltimore, Washington, D.C., Chicago, New Haven, Des Moines, and Newark. Among the worst occurred during the summer of 1967 in Detroit; an estimated fifteen thousand troops and police were required to quell that uprising, which left forty-three dead and a thousand injured.

This level of violence was something new; it overshadowed anything the South had ever experienced. As authorities later tried to analyze what went wrong in Watts, they realized that much of the rioting was directed against symbols of white authority—policemen, firemen—and not simply white people. However, though the causes for the riots were complex and varied, a 1968 report by the National Advisory Commission on Civil Disorder concluded that "White racism is essentially responsible for the explosive mixture which has been accumulating in our cities since the end of World War

II."[87] The report also suggested that in the majority of cases, "What the rioters appeared to be seeking was fuller participation in the social order and the material benefits enjoyed by the majority of American citizens. Rather than rejecting the American system, they were anxious to obtain a place for themselves in it."[88]

But the nation did not appear ready to absorb blacks into its mainstream in the mid-1960s. Instead, the report warned, "Our nation is moving toward two societies, one black, one white—separate and unequal."[89]

Police patrol past a dead man in Watts after the 1965 riots. Blacks resorted to violence after growing frustrated with the failure of nonviolent tactics.

Not everyone was surprised or appalled by the findings. By this time, a growing number of black militants had given up on the idea of peaceful coexistence with whites. Instead, they advocated a policy of black separatism from the rest of American society. Many radicals spoke of a coming revolution and identified themselves with black Africans and other oppressed peoples in underdeveloped countries of the Third World.

The Black Separatists

One of the leading separatists was an intense, intelligent, and articulate ex-convict called Malcolm X. While in prison, he had converted to an antiwhite religious sect, the Black Muslims. Transformed by the experience, Malcolm changed his last name from Little to X (to cast off his "slave" name) and spent the remainder of his prison sentence trying to improve his intellect by reading the works of great thinkers.

After his release, Malcolm X became a fiery spokesman for the Black Muslims. He espoused a doctrine that combined hatred toward whites, racial purity and segregation, black pride, and armed self-defense. He had no use for Martin Luther King's brand of nonviolence, which he believed was naïve and ineffective. Instead, he urged blacks to band together, separate from white America—even if that meant a separate black homeland—and struggle to lift themselves up and lead righteous lives.

Young urban blacks thrilled to Malcolm X's speeches. Though critics condemned many of his views as dangerously extreme, many also had to admit that the Black Muslims' teachings of self-discipline

Although Malcolm X would later recant, the civil rights leader initially espoused a doctrine of hatred toward whites, racial purity, black pride, and armed self-defense.

and pride, coupled with a powerful belief in God, had a tremendous uplifting effect that redeemed many human lives that otherwise would have been lost to drugs, alcohol, and crime.

Malcolm soon broke away from the Black Muslims, however, and began searching for new ideas to justify Black Power. Eventually many of his more militant views softened as a result of his pilgrimage to Mecca, the holy city of Muslims. Here, he witnessed Muslims from many lands praying and worshiping together as brothers and sisters. He returned to the United States with a conviction that finding common ground with whites—especially younger whites—was possible. He also took a more conciliatory approach toward civil rights leaders.

But Malcolm's change of attitude also brought him condemnation. Many young urban blacks felt he had betrayed them by drifting away from his earlier radical positions. Black Muslims were also displeased. Soon, Malcolm began receiving disturbing death threats. In Harlem, on February 21, 1965, as he began to address a rally of his Organization for Afro-American Unity, three black males gunned the black leader down in plain view of his wife and children. Malcolm's death sparked several days of tension and controversy within the black community. Some suspected the Black Muslims of masterminding the assassination. Others wondered if the CIA or the FBI was responsible for eliminating someone who had antagonized white society for so long.

Across America many blacks grieved. At Malcolm's funeral, black actor and activist Ossie Davis called the slain leader "a prince—our own shining prince—who did not hesitate to die, because he loved us so."[90]

With the passing of Malcolm X, others picked up the banner of separatism, including SNCC's firebrand leader, Stokely Carmichael. Under his fervent leadership, SNCC renounced its old civil rights agenda, and in 1966 the group's black members began pressuring whites to leave the organization so that it could become an all-black enterprise. Black Power, not integration, was SNCC's expressed goal. And its salute was the clenched fist.

"People ought to understand . . . we were never fighting for the right to integrate, we were fighting against white supremacy,"[91] Carmichael told a university audience at Berkeley in October 1966.

Also in that year, CORE abandoned its long-held goal of integration and advocated Black Power instead. White supporters were shocked and hurt by this philosophical about-face and began withdrawing their membership.

What was Black Power? As the term was analyzed in countless articles, books, and media broadcasts, the phrase came to mean many things. In its most constructive form, Black Power referred to the act of taking pride in the Negro race and African heritage and participating in the electoral process.

But to black extremists such as the Black Muslims, Black Power meant seeking physical separation from whites. A National Conference on Black Power held at Newark, New Jersey, in July 1967 passed a resolution calling for dividing America into a "homeland for black Americans and a homeland for white Americans."[92]

Many militant blacks deliberately aroused white fears by using separatism and Black Power to express rage, anger, and hatred against whites. The Black Panthers, for example, a militant armed group in Oakland, California, openly declared a willingness to use weapons. They brandished them, for example, when they shad-

After the death of Malcolm X, SNCC leader Stokely Carmichael took up the cause of black separatism.

owed white police patrols in their neighborhoods. They were prepared, they said, to use force to stop acts of police brutality.

But Black Panthers also spoke of revenge. Explained Huey Newton, Panther minister of defense:

The Ballot or the Bullet

In his "Address to a Meeting in New York, 1964" which appears in Documentary History of the Modern Civil Rights Movement, *edited by Peter B. Levy, Malcolm X explains why many blacks felt they had no choice but to turn to violence.*

"When the black man starts reaching out for what America says are his rights, the black man feels that he is within his rights—when he becomes the victim of brutality by those who are depriving him of his rights—to do whatever necessary to protect himself. . . .

And the only way without bloodshed that this [revolution] can be brought about is that the black man has to be given full use of the ballot in every one of the 50 states. But if the black man doesn't get the ballot, then you are going to be faced with another man who forgets the ballot and starts using the bullet."

Kill the slavemaster, destroy him utterly, move against him with [unyielding strength]. Break his oppressive power by any means necessary. . . . The choice offered by the heirs of Malcolm is to repudiate the oppressor . . . or face a merciless, speedy and most timely execution for treason.[93]

Such talk terrified whites and prompted the FBI and many police departments across the nation to attempt to infiltrate and destroy Black Panther cells everywhere.

The Panthers' cry of revolution also troubled many black Americans, including top leaders of the nation's mainstream civil rights groups such as the SCLC and the NAACP. These officials believed the Black Power movement did little except divide and weaken the civil rights coalition. In addition, they feared radical demands from Black Power advocates would trigger a violent white backlash. Ominous signs were already appearing; in 1966, for example, a mob of twelve hundred whites attacked blacks on the streets of Baltimore with cries of revenge.

Civil rights leaders were blunt in their criticism of black radicals. "The problem with hatred and violence is that they intensify the fears of the white majority, and leave them less ashamed of their prejudices towards the Negroes,"[94] King pointed out. NAACP leader Roy Wilkins called Black Power "Wicked fanaticism [that brought] in the end only black death."[95]

Such criticism of Black Power did little to stop it. In fact, the more controversy it created, the more attractive it became to the news media. Realizing that the civil rights movement was in danger of being ambushed by radicals, King decided it was time for his forces to recapture the limelight. And the best way to accomplish this, he said, was to organize another huge march.

Trying to Hold On to the Movement

To draw national attention to the economic woes of African Americans, King planned

Black Panthers give the Black Power salute outside their all-black "Liberation School" in San Francisco in 1969.

A soldier directs traffic in the aftermath of the riots following Martin Luther King's assassination.

to lead a massive "Poor People's March" on Washington. But first, he had a promise to keep: to make a trip to Memphis to demonstrate his support for a garbage workers' strike in that city. It was a fatal decision.

On April 4, 1968, while standing on a balcony of the Lorraine Motel in Memphis, a gunshot rang out. Instantly, King fell, the right side of his jaw and neck torn away. An undercover policeman tried hard to stop the bleeding with a towel, as King's aides rushed to his side. Reverend Ralph Abernathy dropped to his knees and tried to console his old friend: "Martin, this is me, this is Ralph, this is Ralph. Don't be afraid."[96]

A moment later, Andrew Young, an SCLC staffer and future UN ambassador, felt King's pulse and exclaimed, "Oh, my God, my God, it's all over."[97]

Abernathy cried, "No, it's not over. Don't you *ever* say that."[98]

But it was nearly over. An hour later at St. Joseph's Hospital the leader of the civil rights movement—a man who preached that America's racial divide could be breached by Christian love—was pronounced dead.

The murder of King triggered an immediate outburst of grief—and vengeance. Across America, mobs of blacks rioted, burned, and looted buildings and residences. Washington, D.C., was illuminated by an estimated seven hundred fires. Though rioters often burned white-owned stores and businesses in the nation's capital and elsewhere, the fires sometimes spread to black-owned enterprises. By the time calm was finally restored, the violence had wrought a terrible toll. Historian Robert Weisbrot summarizes:

> [The riot] cost nine lives in Washington. Nationally the toll was forty-six, of whom all but five were Negroes, in the most concentrated week of racial violence Americans had ever known. Though no city experienced the level of fury that struck Washington, over 130 lesser riots formed a bitter commemoration of King's murder. Some 2,600 fires exacted property damage of over $100 million, by conservative estimates. The disorders led to 20,000 police arrests and brought 130,000 troops and national guardsmen into domestic combat.[99]

Marchers participate in the Poor People's March on Washington, D.C. Heavy rains, bickering among participants, and rock-throwing gangs plagued the march.

During the week of disorder, Congress focused on an important piece of civil rights legislation. Five years earlier, the assassination of John Kennedy contributed to the passage of the Civil Rights Act of 1964. Now King's death made a similar impact on another bill that had been debated since January 1968. Just six days after King's assassination, the bill was passed. The next day, April 11, President Johnson signed the Civil Rights Act of 1968 into law outlawing discrimination in most kinds of housing.

Despite the loss of King, the SCLC determined to carry out the Poor People's March on Washington as King had planned. The march's new leader was Reverend Ralph Abernathy, King's trusted friend and adviser. He was also the person the fatalistic King hoped would succeed him if assassination came. Many SCLC officials believed Abernathy was the right man for the job. He shared many of King's views and had been deeply involved in the movement since its beginning in Montgomery. Though Abernathy lacked King's refine-

ment, his rural background and friendliness made it easy for him to communicate with common people. Despite his own significant attributes, however, he could not match King's charismatic personality, moral authority, and powerful leadership skills. And without these qualities the next—and last—major civil rights crusade was doomed to failure.

The Poor People's March began on May 2. Its goal was to dramatically highlight the plight of poor people—blacks, Native Americans, Hispanics—and to rally for economic assistance from business and government. Problems plagued this massive undertaking from the start, however. Heavy rains hampered efforts to build a shantytown in Washington, D.C., needed to house the expected thousands of participants. Meanwhile, bickering among the various ethnic groups undermined the attempt to present a solid front to the public. In addition, rock-throwing youth gangs constantly defied their elders' pleas for nonviolence.

As a result of these problems, weeks of rallies and speech making by Abernathy and other leaders failed to fully articulate exactly what actions were needed. Nor did the many demonstrations in the nation's capital succeed in capturing the attention of the general public, big business, or the government. By the end of June, the march ended in disarray and disappointment.

In that same month, the massive manhunt for King's assassin ended in London with the arrest of ex-convict and white racist James Earl Ray. On March 10, 1969, the convicted killer of America's greatest civil rights leader was sentenced to a Tennessee prison for ninety-nine years.

By now the hole created by King's absence was painfully obvious. Perhaps, no other individual could command the loyalty and respect as a national leader that the minister from Dexter Avenue Baptist Church achieved. Many civil rights leaders realized that without King yet another death was imminent—that of the civil rights movement itself.

The Movement Falters

By the late 1960s, Americans were weary of the rioting. Crime, not civil rights, was whites' most pressing concern. Blacks were exhausted too; many were tired of seeing their communities burned and ransacked.

Black separatists were losing support. The radical philosophies of SNCC and CORE proved costly and divisive. Membership and financial contributions started to drop off. Jewish contributors, who had been longtime supporters of the civil rights movement, were especially offended by a rash of anti-Semitic statements from Black Power advocates. Meanwhile, militant groups such as the Black Panthers were disappearing as a result of numerous arrests, wiretaps, and bloody shootouts with law enforcement officers.

But the civil rights movement was also losing its momentum. Though the SCLC and NAACP remained active and true to their governing principles, many of their new members seemed to lack the verve, drive, and dedication that once motivated the founding members.

To some degree, the movement was also undermined by a backlash from the white working class. Having only recently moved out of poverty themselves, many blue-collar whites resented special new federal programs for African Americans. Their discontent helped to prompt both major political parties to become more conservative. The shift became clear in the 1968 presidential election, in which conservative Republican Richard Nixon defeated his Democratic opponent, Hubert Humphrey, a well-known civil rights supporter. Though Nixon did support many civil rights initiatives, he clearly expressed an attitude of coolness toward the movement.

"The new administration promptly applied brakes to federal spending for the advancement of black people . . . and gave other signals that the tide had turned,"[100] observed C. Vann Woodward. This slowing down on civil rights issues was part of Nixon's "Southern Strategy"—a plan to appease whites in the Democratic South and win their political support.

In short, the civil rights movement had peaked. Across the country, blacks and whites who had once worked together in a noble cause began drifting apart. And now the entire nation was left wondering, Just what had this black uprising accomplished?

9 The Legacy of the Civil Rights Movement

Like other mass movements in history, the American civil rights movement left behind a mixed record of successes and disappointments. Positive gains were undeniable, especially in the South. The most obvious is the abolishment of Jim Crow: Today, African Americans have the legally enforceable right to shop, dine, or sleep at public accommodations without fear of reprisals.

Gone too are poll taxes, literacy tests, and other connivances that disenfranchised blacks. Because of these changes, African Americans can now freely exercise their right to vote anywhere in the nation, including the Deep South. Black candidates also continue to win elective offices. Throughout the nation, including the old Confederacy, blacks serve as judges, mayors, county commissioners, and members of city councils and school boards. African Americans also hold offices in state legislatures and the U.S. Congress. In recent decades, two black men, Thurgood Marshall and Clarence Thomas, have been appointed to the Supreme Court. During the 1980s, in Virginia—the very place where North American slavery began—Douglas Wilder became that state's first black governor. The considerable multiracial popular support for General Colin Powell as a possible candidate for the 1996 presiden-

tial elections also revealed America's willingness to place merit over race.

Progress has also been made in the economic sector. Though too many blacks are still trapped in a nightmare world of ghetto violence, drugs, and gangs, millions of African Americans have escaped poverty thanks to personal determination, hard work, and opportunities made possible by civil rights activists. In fact, by the late 1990s, a majority of blacks had joined the American middle class.

Civil rights lawyer Thurgood Marshall was appointed to the Supreme Court. Today, blacks have achieved many of their hard-fought goals.

General Colin Powell's courage and dedication brought him unprecedented popularity.

Despite these improvements, however, many racial problems still plague the nation.

Lingering Troubles

During the last quarter of the twentieth century, the federal government assumed the responsibility for aggressively meeting civil rights goals. For example, it created well-meaning yet contentious racial-preference rules in an attempt to make up for past discrimination against blacks and other minorities. Among other things, these guidelines, commonly called affirmative action programs, require that university admission officials show favoritism to certain minority applicants. Many companies and businesses have faced the same sort of demands when hiring new workers. Government agencies also have had to set aside a certain percentage of contracts for minority firms.

Defenders of such practices believe they are necessary for blacks and other minority groups to overcome setbacks caused by past racism and discrimination. However, critics of affirmative action, including some black leaders, complain the rules are no longer needed and are nothing but a form of "reverse discrimination."

Meanwhile, new troubles have plagued the nation's public schools. One of the most vexing became the forced busing of school children. In 1971 the Supreme Court ruled in *Swann v. Charlotte-Mecklenburg Board of Education* that federal courts had the authority to order busing to desegregate public schools. Since then judges across the nation have ordered many local school districts to use busing to achieve this end.

But these actions have often met stiff resistance, not all of which was racially based. Many parents were upset that their children could not attend schools in their own neighborhood and instead would be bused to distant schools. Over the years, forced busing has proven so unpopular that large numbers of families have either moved away from their school districts altogether or have enrolled their children in private schools.

Busing is also expensive. In fact, by the late 1990s, many school districts, including Prince Georges County, Maryland, which is predominantly black, wanted to eliminate forced busing and use the financial savings to improve education instead.

A Racial Divide

That America is still charged with racial tension became clear in 1992 when a videotape of police officers beating a black motorist, thirty-year-old Rodney King, led to riots in Los Angeles that were reminiscent of the 1965 turbulence in Watts.

In 1995, Americans received another hard lesson in the gulf still separating blacks and whites when a mostly black jury in Los Angeles found African American football celebrity O. J. Simpson not guilty of murdering either his white wife or her white male friend. Although the trial was televised for all to see and assess, public reaction to the jury verdict split largely along racial lines across the nation: Opinion polls repeatedly showed a majority of whites thought Simpson was guilty and a majority of blacks thought he was not.

Although these examples prove racial divisions, black opinion is no longer censored and ignored as it was prior to the civil rights movement. In addition, black leaders still rally for black unity to respond to problems that plague their communities, such as the high number of single-parent households, poverty, and drug use. On October 16, 1995, the nation witnessed another mass gathering of African Americans at the nation's capital for the "Million Man March."

Though many African American women and children attended the event, the vast majority of participants were men—over a million strong, according to organizers of the march. They had come from all across America to show unity and to rally for self-respect. Speakers at the march criticized conditions that still bedeviled blacks, and called upon African American men to publicly commit themselves to improving their own lives, families, and communities.

The leader of this grand assemblage was Louis Farrakhan, a controversial leader of the Nation of Islam, the Black Muslims. Far different from King, whose "I Have a Dream" speech dominated the 1963 March on Washington, Farrakhan was seen by many blacks and whites as a divisive figure who had publicly proclaimed his racial hatred and anti-Semitism. Some black leaders, such as civil rights veteran and congressman John Lewis, refused to attend the event.

Other black leaders, even if they were wary of Farrakhan, attended the march on the grounds that any effort to unify black Americans was sorely needed.

Looters run off with goods from a stereo store during the 1992 Los Angeles riots. Riots began after an all-white jury acquitted white police officers of using excessive force against Rodney King.

Thousands participate in the Million Man March to Washington in 1995. The rally's goal was to unite black men and confirm their commitment to their families and their pledge of self-reliance.

Despite misgivings about Farrakhan, legions of black men left Washington, D.C., that day with a feeling of energy, hope, and pride and vowed to make the nation a better place in which blacks could live.

The Future

And a better life is exactly what the pioneers of the civil rights movement also desired. The crusade they launched accomplished much of what many had hoped for, more than what some expected, and fell short of what others had dreamed.

Though much work was left undone, the civil rights movement clearly achieved something powerful and enduring: It forced the nation to make a collective effort to remedy wrongs of the past and to reexamine its professed, cherished values. And out of that strong, but imperfect, undertaking, came a new willingness across America to create a more just society for all.

Notes

Introduction: A Struggle to Change Hearts and Minds

1. Quoted in Stephen B. Oates, *Let the Trumpet Sound: A Life of Martin Luther King*. New York: HarperPerennial, 1982, p. xxiv.

2. C. Vann Woodward, *The Strange Career of Jim Crow*. New York: Oxford University Press, 1974, p. 9.

Chapter 1: The Roots of the Civil Rights Movement

3. Quoted in Geoffrey C. Ward, *The Civil War*. New York: Knopf, 1990, p. 24.

4. Quoted in Hodding Carter, *The Angry Scar*. Garden City, NY: Doubleday, 1959, p. 52.

5. Quoted in Juan Williams, *Eyes on the Prize*. New York: Viking Penguin, 1987, p. 8.

6. Tim Jacobson, *Heritage of the South*. New York: Crescent Books, 1992, p. 142.

7. Jacobson, *Heritage of the South*, p. 142.

8. Quoted in Dorothy Sterling, *Tear Down the Walls: A History of the American Civil Rights Movement*. Garden City, NY: Doubleday, 1968, p. 87.

9. Quoted in Sterling, *Tear Down the Walls*, p. 76.

10. Quoted in Sterling, *Tear Down the Walls*, p. 69.

11. Quoted in Woodward, *The Strange Career of Jim Crow*, p. 49.

12. Jacobson, *Heritage of the South*, p. 143.

13. Woodward, *The Strange Career of Jim Crow*, p. 48.

14. Quoted in John M. Blum et al., *The National Experience: A History of the United States*. 6th ed. San Diego: Harcourt Brace Jovanovich, 1985, p. 514.

15. Woodward, *The Strange Career of Jim Crow*, p. 80.

16. Dewey W. Grantham, *The South in Modern America: A Region at Odds*. New York: Harper-Perennial, 1994, p. 15.

17. Robert A. Calvert, "Protest Movements," in Charles Reagan Wilson and William Ferris, eds., *Encyclopedia of Southern Culture*. Chapel Hill: University of North Carolina Press, 1989, p. 1,174.

18. Quoted in William Pitt, *We Americans*, vol. 2, *1865 to the Present*. Glenview, IL: Scott, Foresman, 1976, p. 422.

Chapter 2: The Long Night

19. Quoted in William Loren Katz, ed., *Eyewitness: A Living Documentary of the African American Contribution to American History*. New York: Simon & Schuster, 1995, p. 314.

20. Quoted in Albert P. Blaustein and Robert L. Zangrando, eds., *Civil Rights and the American Negro: A Documentary History*. New York: Trident Press, 1968, p. 290.

21. Quoted in Howard Zinn, *A People's History of the United States*. New York: Harper and Row, 1980, p. 340.

22. Quoted in Blaustein and Zangrando, *Civil Rights and the American Negro*, pp. 335–36.

23. Quoted in Blaustein and Zangrando, *Civil Rights and the American Negro*, p. 334.

Chapter 3: Black Attitudes Change

24. W. S. Cash, *The Mind of the South*. New York: Knopf, 1941, p. 317.

25. John Hope Franklin, "Equality Indivisible," *Forum: The Civil Rights Era*, Winter 1994/1995, p. 6.

26. Quoted in Sterling, *Tear Down the Walls*, p. 149.

27. Franklin, "Equality Indivisible," *Forum*, p. 6.

28. Quoted in Zinn, *A People's History of the United States*, p. 440.

29. John Gunther, *Inside U.S.A.* New York: Harper and Brothers, 1947, p. 687.

Chapter 4: The Walls of Segregation Begin to Crack

30. Williams, *Eyes on the Prize*, p. 15.

31. Woodward, *The Strange Career of Jim Crow*, pp. 144–45.

32. Hugh Speer, "The Case of the Century: *Brown v. Board of Education of Topeka*," in *American History*, vol. 2, *Reconstruction Through the Present*. Guilford, CT: Dushkin Publishing Group, 1989, p. 175.

33. Quoted in Speer, "The Case of the Century," p. 176.

34. Quoted in Leon Friedman, ed., *The Civil Rights Reader: Basic Documents of the Civil Rights Movement*. New York: Walker, 1968, pp. 31–32.

35. Quoted in Peter B. Levy, *Documentary History of the Modern Civil Rights Movement*. New York: Greenwood Press, 1992, p. 55.

36. Martin Luther King, "Stride Toward Freedom," in Friedman, *The Civil Rights Reader*, p. 38.

37. Quoted in Levy, *Documentary History of the Modern Civil Rights Movement*, p. 58.

38. Quoted in Williams, *Eyes on the Prize*, p. 82.

39. Andrew Young, *An Easy Burden: The Civil Rights Movement and the Transformation of America*. New York: HarperCollins, 1996, p. 2.

Chapter 5: The Rise of White Militant Resistance

40. Quoted in Williams, *Eyes on the Prize*, p. 38.

41. Quoted in Zinn, *A People's History of the United States*, pp. 438–39.

42. Quoted in Zinn, *A People's History of the United States*, p. 439.

43. Levy, *Documentary History of the Modern Civil Rights Movement*, p. 212.

44. Quoted in Aldon D. Morris, *The Origins of the Civil Rights Movement: Black Communities Organizing for Change*. New York: Collier Macmillan, 1984, p. 29.

45. Morris, *The Origins of the Civil Rights Movement*, p. 30.

46. Quoted in Levy, *Documentary History of the Modern Civil Rights Movement*, p. 214.

47. Quoted in Sara Bullard, ed., *Free at Last: A History of the Civil Rights Movement and Those Who Died in the Struggle*. Montgomery, AL: The Civil Rights Education Project, Southern Poverty Law Center, n.d., p. 36.

48. Quoted in Bullard, *Free at Last*, p. 41.

49. Quoted in Williams, *Eyes on the Prize*, p. 99.

50. Quoted in Williams, *Eyes on the Prize*, p. 100.

51. Quoted in Williams, *Eyes on the Prize*, p. 100.

52. Quoted in Katz, *Eyewitness*, p. 456.

53. Woodward, *The Strange Career of Jim Crow*, p. 167.

Chapter 6: Confrontations

54. Quoted in Bullard, *Free at Last*, p. 18.

55. Quoted in Levy, *Documentary History of the Modern Civil Rights Movement*, p. 67.

56. Quoted in Levy, *Documentary History of the Modern Civil Rights Movement*, p. 67.

57. Quoted in Robert Weisbrot, *Freedom Bound*. New York: W. W. Norton, 1990, p. 57.

58. Quoted in Williams, *Eyes on the Prize*, p. 149.

59. Quoted in Friedman, *The Civil Rights Reader*, p. 56.

60. Quoted in Williams, *Eyes on the Prize*, p. 146.

61. Quoted in Bullard, *Free at Last*, p. 52.

62. Quoted in *Eyewitnesses and Others, Readings in American History*, vol. 2, *1865 to the Present*. Austin, TX: Holt, Rinehart, and Winston, 1991, p. 368.

63. Quoted in Sterling, *Tear Down the Walls*, p. 205.

64. Quoted in Friedman, *The Civil Rights Reader*, p. 66.

65. Williams, *Eyes on the Prize*, p. 198.

66. Quoted in Friedman, *The Civil Rights Reader*, p. 112.

67. Quoted in Bullard, *Free at Last*, p. 60.

68. Quoted in Bullard, *Free at Last*, p. 61.

69. Quoted in Weisbrot, *Freedom Bound*, p. 88.

Chapter 7: Battle for the Ballot

70. Quoted in Friedman, *The Civil Rights Reader*, p. 194.

71. Benjamin Muse, *The American Negro Revolution: From Nonviolence to Black Power, 1960–1961.* Bloomington: Indiana University Press, 1973, p. 140.

72. Quoted in Bullard, *Free at Last*, p. 64.

73. Quoted in Muse, *The American Negro Revolution*, p. 144.

74. Muse, *The American Negro Revolution*, p. 142.

75. Quoted in Bullard, *Free at Last*, p. 73.

76. Quoted in Muse, *The American Negro Revolution*, p. 166.

77. Muse, *The American Negro Revolution*, p. 166.

78. Quoted in Bullard, *Free at Last*, p. 75.

79. Quoted in Muse, *The American Negro Revolution*, p. 169.

80. Quoted in Friedman, *The Civil Rights Reader*, p. 85.

81. Quoted in Muse, *The American Negro Revolution*, p. 172.

82. Zinn, *A People's History of the United States*, p. 448.

83. Renata Adler, "The Meredith Mississippi March (1966)," in Friedman, *The Civil Rights Reader*, p. 105.

Chapter 8: The Movement Splinters

84. Quoted in Katz, *Eyewitness*, p. 475.

85. Pitt, *We Americans*, p. 745.

86. "Report of the National Advisory Commission on Civil Disorder," in Friedman, *The Civil Rights Reader*, p. 354.

87. "Report of the National Advisory Commission on Civil Disorder," in Friedman, *The Civil Rights Reader*, p. 347.

88. "Report of the National Advisory Commission on Civil Disorder," in Friedman, *The Civil Rights Reader*, p. 351.

89. "Report of the National Advisory Commission on Civil Disorder," in Friedman, *The Civil Rights Reader*, p. 347.

90. Quoted in Weisbrot, *Freedom Bound*, p. 161.

91. Stokely Carmichael, "Berkeley Speech (October 1966)," James R. Andrews and David Zarefsky, eds., *Contemporary American Voices: Significant Speeches in American History, 1945–Present.* White Plains, NY: Longman, 1992, p. 102.

92. Quoted in Muse, *The American Negro Revolution*, pp. 298–99.

93. Quoted in Blum et al., *The National Experience*, p. 832.

94. Quoted in Blum et al., *The National Experience*, p. 833.

95. Quoted in Muse, *The American Negro Revolution*, p. 243.

96. Quoted in Oates, *Let the Trumpet Sound*, p. 490.

97. Quoted in Oates, *Let the Trumpet Sound*, p. 490.

98. Quoted in Oates, *Let the Trumpet Sound*, p. 490.

99. Weisbrot, *Freedom Bound*, p. 270.

100. Woodward, *The Strange Career of Jim Crow*, p. 211.

For Further Reading

Mark Davis, *Malcolm X: Another Side of the Movement.* Englewood Cliffs, NJ: Silver Burdett, 1990. A fast-moving and well-rounded biography of a controversial black nationalist.

James Haskins, *The Life and Death of Martin Luther King, Jr.* New York: Lothrop, Lee & Shephard, 1977. A highly readable account of King's life and assassination.

Debra Hess, *Thurgood Marshall: The Fight for Equal Justice.* Englewood Cliffs, NJ: Silver Burdett, 1990. Another well-written biography of the first black to become a Supreme Court justice.

Dr. Howard O. Lindsey, *A History of Black America.* Secaucus, NJ: Chartwell Books, 1994. A richly illustrated history of African Americans for the general reader.

Pat Rediger, *Great African Americans in Civil Rights.* New York: Crabtree, 1996. A slim quick-reference volume of leading personalities in the civil rights movement.

Works Consulted

James R. Andrews and David Zarefsky, eds., *Contemporary American Voices: Significant Speeches in American History, 1945–Present.* White Plains, NY: Longman, 1992. A collection of primary sources.

Albert P. Blaustein and Robert L. Zangrando, eds., *Civil Rights and the American Negro: A Documentary History.* New York: Trident Press, 1968. A compilation of documents arranged in chronological order.

John M. Blum, William S. McFeely, Edmund S. Morgan, Arthur M. Schlesinger Jr., Kenneth M. Stampp, and C. Vann Woodward, eds., *The National Experience: A History of the United States.* 6th ed. San Diego: Harcourt Brace Jovanovich, 1985. A college-level textbook.

Sara Bullard, ed., *Free at Last: A History of the Civil Rights Movement and Those Who Died in the Struggle.* Montgomery, AL: The Civil Rights Education Project, Southern Poverty Law Center, n.d. A readable, concise history in booklet form with an abundance of photographs and poignant biographies of murdered civil rights workers.

Hodding Carter, *The Angry Scar.* Garden City, NY: Doubleday, 1959. A comprehensive, scholarly work on Reconstruction by a Pulitzer Prize–winning editor.

W. S. Cash, *The Mind of the South.* New York: Knopf, 1941. This oft-cited classic study examines the mentality of white southerners from Reconstruction to the late 1930s.

———, ed., *Civil Rights Decisions of the United States Supreme Court: The 20th Century.* San Diego: Excellent Books, 1994. A collection of transcripts of major court decisions.

W. E. B. Du Bois, *The Souls of Black Folk.* New York: Dodd, Mead, 1979. An important, turn-of-the-century collection of essays and sketches by a notable African American leader.

Eyewitnesses and Others: Readings in American History. Vol. 2, *1865 to the Present.* Austin, TX: Holt, Rinehart, and Winston, 1991. A compilation of primary sources.

John Hope Franklin, "Equality Indivisible," *Forum, The Civil Rights Era,* Winter 1994/1995. A quarterly publication of the Florida Humanities Council.

Leon Friedman, ed., *The Civil Rights Reader: Basic Documents of the Civil Rights Movement.* New York: Walker, 1968. A collection of essays, official reports, and documents concerning civil rights from 1947 to 1968.

Dewey W. Grantham, *The South in Modern America: A Region at Odds.* New York: HarperPerennial, 1994. A scholarly history.

Rebecca Brooks Gruver, *American History, Third Edition Volume I: to 1877.* Reading, MA: Addison-Wesley, 1976. A college text.

John Gunther, *Inside U.S.A.* New York: Harper and Brothers, 1947. A leading journalist's fact-filled, in-depth look into the social fabric of the United States at the end of World War II.

Tim Jacobson, *Heritage of the South*. New York: Crescent Books, 1992. A history of the South for the general reader.

William Loren Katz, ed., *Eyewitness: A Living Documentary of the African American Contribution to American History*. New York: Simon & Schuster, 1995. A collection of primary sources linked by a useful and well-written narrative.

Peter B. Levy, *Documentary History of the Modern Civil Rights Movement*. New York: Greenwood Press, 1992. An anthology of book excerpts, essays, and other passages from observers and participants in the civil rights movement.

Robert James Maddox, ed., *American History*. Vol. 2, *Reconstruction Through the Present*. Guilford, CT: Dushkin Publishing Group, 1989. A collection of scholarly articles on American history.

Aldon D. Morris, *The Origins of the Civil Rights Movement: Black Communities Organizing for Change*. New York: Collier Macmillan, 1984. A scholarly work on the underlying causes of the movement.

Benjamin Muse, *The American Negro Revolution: From Nonviolence to Black Power, 1960–1961*. Bloomington: Indiana University Press, 1973. A very readable and interesting history.

Stephen B. Oates, *Let the Trumpet Sound: A Life of Martin Luther King*. New York: HarperPerennial, 1982. A highly acclaimed biography for all serious readers.

Rosa Parks with Gregory J. Reed, *Quiet Strength: The Faith, the Hope, and the Heart of a Woman Who Changed a Nation*. Grand Rapids, MI: Zondervan, 1994. A collection of memories, reflections, and opinions.

William Pitt, *We Americans*. Vol. 2, *1865 to the Present*. Glenview, IL: Scott, Foresman, 1976. A college-level history.

Jo Ann Gibson Robinson, *The Montgomery Bus Boycott and the Women Who Started It: The Memoir of Jo Ann Gibson Robinson*. Knoxville: University of Tennessee Press, 1987. A very readable and informative firsthand history of the famous boycott written by one of its organizers.

Dorothy Sterling, *Tear Down the Walls: A History of the American Civil Rights Movement*. Garden City, NY: Doubleday, 1968. A well-written history that supplies a comprehensive background on the forces that led to the civil rights movement.

Geoffrey C. Ward, *The Civil War*. New York: Knopf, 1990. A very readable history for the general reader with excellent illustrations and photographs.

Robert Weisbrot, *Freedom Bound*. New York: W. W. Norton, 1990. This comprehensive and well-written history covers the civil rights movement to the Reagan years.

Juan Williams, *Eyes on the Prize*. New York: Viking Penguin, 1987. A highly readable book with many primary source quotations that covers the civil rights movement from 1954 to 1965.

Charles Reagan Wilson and William Ferris, eds., *Encyclopedia of Southern Culture*. Chapel Hill: University of North Carolina Press, 1989. A fascinating compilation of essays and articles about the South for both the scholar and the general reader.

C. Vann Woodward, *The Strange Career of Jim Crow*. New York: Oxford University Press, 1974. A concise, scholarly treatment of the origins and consequences of the Jim Crow laws by an esteemed historian.

Andrew Young, *An Easy Burden: The Civil Rights Movement and the Transformation of America.* New York: HarperCollins, 1996. This personal account by a civil rights leader and political figure provides general readers and scholars alike with a well-written and interesting history of the modern civil rights movement.

Howard Zinn, *A People's History of the United States.* New York: Harper and Row, 1980. An unorthodox history told from perspectives that are often overlooked by mainstream writers.

Index

Abernathy, Ralph, 53,
109–10
Adler, Renata, 99
affirmative action, 113
African Americans
achieve citizenship, 17
changing attitudes of,
after World War I,
39–45
disenfranchisement of,
29–31
migrate to northern
cities, 27–28, 40–41
see also Black *headings*
Alabama Christian Move-
ment for Human Rights,
82
amendments to Constitu-
tion
Thirteenth (abolished
slavery), 14
Fourteenth (blacks now
citizens), 17
Fifteenth (blacks' right to
vote), 19
Twenty-fourth (poll tax
banned), 97
American Nazi Party, 100
Anderson, Marian, 41–42
Association of Citizens'
Councils, 64

Barnett, Ross, 79–80, 83
Beveridge, Albert J., 27
Birmingham, Alabama
murder of black girls in,
87
violence and bombings
in, 81–84
Black Codes, 16–17
Black Muslims (Nation of
Islam), 105, 114

Black Panthers, 107–108, 111
Black Power, 99, 105–109
clenched fist sign, 106
defined, 107
Blossom (Arkansas school
superintendent), 69
Bowers, Sam, 90
Branton, Wiley, 66
Brotherhood of Sleeping
Car Porters, 42–43
Brown, Linda, 50–51
Brown, Oliver, 50
Brown v. Board of Education
(nonsegregated educa-
tion), 50–52
Bryant, Roy, 65
bus boycott, (Montgomery,
Alabama), 50–57
busing issue, pros and cons,
113
Byrd, Harry F., 63

Calvert, Robert A., 25
Carmichael, Stokely,
99–101, 106–107
Castle, Doris, 75
Catholic Interracial
Council, 88
Chaney, James, 91
Chicago Freedom Move-
ment, 102
Christian Civil League (hate
group), 65
citizens' councils, 64–66
"Civil Disobedience"
(Thoreau), 55
civil rights, defined, 10
Civil Rights Acts
of 1866, 17
of 1875, 21
of 1964, 88, 110
of 1968, 110

Civil Rights Cases of 1883,
26
civil rights movement
in Birmingham, Alabama,
81–84
birth of, 33–35
black migration aids,
40–41
black separatists (Black
Power) and, 99,
105–109
confrontations during,
73–88
at sit-ins, 73–74
Freedom Riders and,
74–79
Great Depression and,
41–42
important dates in, 8–9
legacy of, 112–15
Little Rock showdown,
66–71
March on Washington,
85–87
Montgomery bus boycott,
50–57
national resistance to
school desegregation,
71–72
Oxford, Mississippi,
fighting in, 79–81
Project C, 82–84
rising violence and, 83–84
roots of, 13–28
Selma, Alabama, and,
92–93
march to Montgomery,
93–98
splinters and falters,
100–11
summers of rage and,
104–105

television's impact on,
    11–12, 70
World War I and, 37–38
World War II and, 42–44
Civil War
    impact on South, 15–16
    Reconstruction period,
    15–21
Clark, Jim, 93–94
Cloven, Claudette, 53
Committee on Civil Rights
    (Truman), 44–45
Communist Party, 61
Congress of Racial Equality.
    See CORE
Connor, Eugene "Bull,"
    81–82
Constitution, U.S. *See* amend-
    ments to Constitution
CORE (Congress of Racial
    Equality)
    founded, 46
    Freedom Riders, 74–76,
    78
    switched to advocate
    Black Power, 106
Council of Federated
    Organizations (COFO),
    90
Cowling, Eli, 76
Crisis (NAACP publication),
    38

Daughters of the American
    Revolution, 41
Davies, Ronald N., 66–67
Davis, Ossie, 106
Dee, Henry, 91
disenfranchisement
    methods, 29–30
Dixon, E. D., 53–55
Doar, John, 95
Du Bois, W. E. B., 34–35, 38
Durr, Virginia, 54, 57

Eastland, James, 60

Eckford, Elizabeth, 67–69
Eisenhower, Dwight, 69–72
Emancipation Proclama-
    tion, 14
Evers, Medgar, 84
Executive Order 8802,
    42–43

Farmer, James, 78
Farrakhan, Louis, 114–15
Faubus, Orville, 66, 68–69,
    71
Fifteenth Amendment
    (blacks' right to vote), 19
Fourteenth Amendment
    (blacks now citizens), 17
Freedom Riders, 74–79
    map, 79
Frye, Marquette, 104

Gaines, Lloyd Lionel, 48
Gandhi, Mohandas, 46, 55
Goodman, Andrew, 91
Grant, Ulysses S., 18, 20
Great Depression, 41–42
Guihard, Paul, 80–81
Gunther, John, 45

Hayes, Rutherford B., 22
Henry, Aaron, 89
Herndon, Angelo, 61–62
Houston, Charles, 47
Howe, Louisa Holt, 50–51
Hughes, Genevieve, 76
Humphrey, Hubert, 111
Humphreys, Benjamin G., 14

"I Have a Dream" speech
    (King), 85–86

Jackson, Jimmie Lee, 93
Jewish Anti-Defamation
    League, 88
Jim Crow
    Civil Rights Act of 1964
    ends segregation, 88

early legal attacks on,
    46–50
expands post–World War
    I, 39–40
at federal level, 35–36
international scrutiny of,
    44–45
laws, 31–35
post–Civil War, in North, 18
Johnson, Andrew, recon-
    struction and, 15–17
Johnson, Frank M., 94
Johnson, Lyndon Baines,
    88, 110
    Selma-to-Montgomery
    march and, 94–95, 97

Kennedy, John F., 74, 85, 87
    assassination of, 87–88
    intervention in South by,
    77, 80, 83–84
Kennedy, Robert, 78, 80
King, A. D., 84
King, Coretta, 88
King, Martin Luther, Jr., 10
    arrests, 56, 82
    assassination of, 109
    awarded Nobel Peace
    Prize, 93
    at Birmingham, 82–84
    Chicago Freedom
    Movement, 102
    "I Have a Dream" speech,
    85–86
    "Letter from a
    Birmingham Jail," 82
    Montgomery bus boycott
    and, 53–57
    rise of, 57–58
    Selma-to-Montgomery
    march and, 93–98
King, Rodney, 114
Kirk, George W., 22
Ku Klux Klan, 18–22, 63, 65
    disbanded in 1873, 21
    laws against, 19

power of, 22
rebirth and growth after
World War I, 39
rise of, 18–21

Lee, George, 65
"Letter from a Birmingham
Jail" (King), 82
Lewis, John, 114
Lincoln, Abraham, 14, 15
Lingo, Al, 94
literacy tests, as disenfran-
chisement, 29
Little, Malcolm. *See*
Malcolm X
Little Rock (AR) showdown,
66–71
Liuzzo, Viola Gregg, 96–97
Long, Howard H., 38
Long Night, 29–45
Loyalty (Liberty) Leagues,
19, 25
Lynch, Connie, 87
lynchings, 45, 65
numbers of, 30
as target of NAACP, 35

Malcolm X, 105–107
Mann, Woodrow, 69
March on Washington
(1963), 85–87
March on Washington
Movement (1942), 44
Margold, Nathan Ross, 47
Margold Report, 47
Marshall, Burke, 83–84
Marshall, Thurgood, 48–49,
66, 112
McCain, Franklin, 73
McLaurin, George, 49
McLaurin v. Oklahoma
(equal education), 48–49
McNair, Chris, 87
Meredith, James, 79, 83
Walk Against Fear and,
98–99

MIA (Montgomery
Improvement
Association), 53–57
Milam, J. W., 65
militant resistance
black, rise of, 74
see also Black Power
white, 59–72
white councils, 64–66
Miller, Orloff, 94
Million Man March, 114–15
Mississippi Freedom
Democrats (MFD), 92
Mississippi Summer
Freedom Project, 90–92
Montgomery, Alabama
bus boycott, 50–57
MIA, 53–57
Moore, Charles, 91
Moses, Robert, 90
Mothers' League of Little
Rock Central High
School, 66
Murray, Donald G., 48

NAACP (National
Association for the
Advancement of Colored
People)
disapproves of Black
Power movement, 108
drive to destroy, 63–64
formed, 35
grows after World War I,
41
sues school boards, 62–63
National Advisory Commis-
sion on Civil Disorder
(1968), 104–105
National Afro-American
Council, 35
National Association for the
Advancement of Colored
People. *See* NAACP
National Conference on
Black Power, 107

National Council of
Churches, 88, 90
National Equal Rights
League, 21
National Organization of
Colored Women, 35
Nation of Islam (Black
Muslims), 105, 114
Newton, Huey, 107–108
Niagara Movement, 35
Nixon, Richard, 111
Nobel Peace Prize, 93

Organization for Afro-
American Unity, 106
Oxford, Mississippi, fighting
in, 79–81

Pale Faces (white militia),
19
Parks, Rosa, 52–55, 57
Patterson, John, 78
Peck, Jim, 76
Plessy, Homer, 26
Plessy v. Ferguson (separate
but equal), 26
legal attacks on, 47–52
overturned, 52
poll tax, as disenfranchisement, 29
Poor People's March,
109–10
Populist Party, 24–26
Powell, Colin, 112–13
Project C, 82–84
property ownership, as
disenfranchisement, 30

Quakers, 88

race distinction vs. race
discrimination, 26
Rainey, Lawrence, 90–91
Randolph, A. Philip, 42–44,
85
Ray, James Earl, 111

Reconstruction period, 15–21
  Black Codes, 16–17
  ended, 21–23
  Loyalty (Liberty) Leagues during, 25
Red Shirts (white militia), 19
Reebs, James J., 94
reverse discrimination, 113
Robinson, Jo Ann, 52–54
Roosevelt, Eleanor, 41–42
Roosevelt, Franklin Delano, 41–43
Rustin, Bayard, 85, 102

school busing, pros and cons, 113
Schurz, Carl, 14
Schwerner, Michael, 91
SCLC. *See* Southern Christian Leadership Conference
Selma-to-Montgomery march, 92–98
  George Wallace and, 94–96
  Lyndon Johnson and, 94–95, 97
separate-but-equal ruling, 26
separatists, black, 105–109
Shuttlesworth, Fred, 82
Simpson, O. J., 114
sit-in, at Greensboro Woolworth, 73–74
slaves
  first in New World, 13
  had no rights, 13–14
  slavery abolished, 14
Smith, Lamar, 65
SNCC (Student Non-violent Coordinating Committee) formed, 74

urges whites to leave organization, 106
Southern Christian Leadership Conference (SCLC)
  disapproves of Black Power, 108
  formed, 58
Southern Manifesto, 63, 70
Southern Strategy, 111
Speer, Hugh, 50
Student Non-violent Coordinating Committee. *See* SNCC
Supreme Court, rules that slaves have no rights, 13–14
Swann v. Charlotte-Mecklenburg Board (school busing), 113
Sweatt v. Painter (equal education), 48–49

television
  Freedom Riders and, 77
  impact on civil rights movement, 11–12, 103–104
  Little Rock and, 70
Thirteenth Amendment (abolished slavery), 14
Thomas, Clarence, 112
Thoreau, Henry David, 55
Till, Emmett, 65
Trotter, Monroe, 36
Truman, Harry, 44–45
Tuskeegee Institute, 34
Twenty-fourth Amendment (poll tax banned), 97

Urban League, 41

vigilantism
  lynchings in South and, 30

white groups develop, 19–21
voting, 87–99
  Mississippi Summer Freedom Project, 90–92
  see also disenfranchisement methods
Voting Rights Act of 1965, 97, 104

Walk Against Fear, 98–99
Wallace, George, 84, 87
  Selma-to-Montgomery march and, 94–96
Warren, Earl, 51–52
Washington, Booker T., 34
Watson, Tom, 24
Watts riot, 104–105
White, George H., 30–31
White Christians (hate group), 65
white councils, 64–66
White Knights (hate group), 90
white militant resistance, rise of, 59–72
Wilder, Douglas, 112
Wilkins, Roy, 108
Wilson, Woodrow, 36–37
Women's Political Council (Montgomery), 52
Woolworth's sit-in (Greensboro), 73–74
World War I
  changing black attitudes after, 39–45
  impact on civil rights movement, 37–38
World War II, impact on civil rights movement, 42–44

Young, Andrew, 109

Picture Credits

Cover photo: Archive Photos

AP/Wide World Photos, 50, 57

Archive Photos, 19, 29, 34, 67, 71, 98, 105, 107, 113, 114, 115

Chicago Historical Society, Prints and Photographs Department, 31

Corbis-Bettmann, 64

Culver Pictures, 23

FDR Library, 41

Library of Congress, 10, 11, 13, 15, 17, 20, 27, 32, 35, 37, 40, 42, 45, 46, 47, 49, 55, 61, 62, 75, 77, 81, 84, 85, 86, 87, 88, 89, 106, 109, 110, 112

North Wind Picture Archives, 14

Shomburg Center for Research in Black Culture, 51, 58, 60

Stock Montage, 21

UPI/Corbis-Bettmann, 65, 73, 78, 81, 82, 91, 92, 93, 96, 102, 103, 108

About the Author

John M. Dunn is a freelance writer and high school history teacher. He has taught in Georgia, Florida, North Carolina, and Germany. As a writer and journalist, he has published over 250 articles and stories in more than 20 periodicals, as well as scripts for audiovisual productions and a children's play. His books—*The Russian Revolution, The Relocation of the North American Indian, The Spread of Islam,* and *Advertising*—were published by Lucent Books. He lives with his wife and two daughters in Ocala, Florida.